OXFORDSHIRE

A LOOK AT THE PAST

Hilary L. Turner

Plotwood
Press

Published by
Plotwood Press
5 Whinbush Avenue, Allenton, Derby DE24 9DQ England

ISBN 0 9529920 0 0

Acknowledgements

My thanks go to Sue and Jim Eaglesham, Lindy Rawling and Martin Sheppard for encourage-
ment as they read the text in various stages; to James Campbell for suggesting the idea; to the
county's many researchers; to the staff of the Local Studies Centre in the Westgate Library,
Oxford; to John Clare for the use of his photograph of Kelmscott. Most of all I wish to thank
Michael Leiserach for the combination of constructive comment and business acumen that made
this book a reality.

Design and production by: Dick Richardson, Country Books, Little Longstone, Derbyshire DE45 1NN, England.

Colour origination by: GA Graphics, Stamford, Lincolnshire PE9 2RB.

Printed by: MFP Design & Print, Stretford, Manchester M32 0JT.

Cartography by: Mark Titterton Design, Ashbourne, Derbyshire DE6 1BH

Contents

List of Illustrations

Cover Photograph
The chancel doorway, Shellingford Church

Introduction

"All the countryside is open, dull and disagreeable, nor does vigorous cultivation of the earth make any amends for these unpleasing circumstances; the crops were generally very poor and mostly full of weeds."

Looking at Oxfordshire only from the M40 or the A34, the county's two major roads, today's traveller might be tempted to agree with these words of the eighteenth-century agricultural scientist, Arthur Young, who crisscrossed the area on horseback. Nevertheless, his comment was scarcely fair when it was made; it is certainly not true now. Few who abandon the present highways for the winding lanes of the Saxon settlers or a walk along the windswept prehistoric Ridgeway track are likely to agree. The countryside is very obviously productive, its villages uniformly prosperous. The near disappearance of rural poverty is one of the greatest changes of this century. Each generation has made some contribution to the landscape. This book aims to trace those changes, from prehistoric times to the present day. Each change reveals a new way of life, sometimes also new beliefs and customs; each has contributed to the appearance of the county today.

Oxfordshire is rich in the background to the daily life of the poorer members of society and in monuments to lost institutions. Some are to be found in unexpected places: Chipping Norton's Workhouse now forms part of a residential estate; Thame's of a college; Abingdon's nineteenth-century gaol is now an Arts and Sports Centre; the guesthouses of Bruern and Godstow abbeys are both public houses, as are the almshouses of Sir John Golafre at Fyfield. Manor houses have made good hotels, for example, at Banbury and Weston on the Green; another was used until recently as an antiquarian bookshop. Two of Oxford city's churches have been adapted into college libraries. A barn of Abingdon Abbey is now a church and one of its granges survives as Sutton Courtenay 'Abbey'; another stands at Culham. A nonconformist chapel in Banbury serves as the entrance to a shopping arcade.

The present area known as Oxfordshire is the artificial creation of the 1974 Boundary Commission. It was achieved by adding a substantial part of Berkshire, known now as the Vale of the White Horse, to the area known as Oxfordshire since before the Norman Conquest. Still a sore point for those who remember the historic divisions, the amalgamation emphasises the fact that the region enjoys a certain unity because it corresponds to a clearly recognisable geographical area, defined by high ground to the north divided by a river system flowing to the south; this is the Oxford Region.

Landlocked in the centre of England, the Oxford region has long been the meeting place of influences seen more strongly beyond its boundaries. Scenically, the county is not dramatic. Most of the land lies below the 700 foot (215 m) contour, much of it apparently level. It has, however, a varied geology; within just a few miles vegetation, agriculture, industry and housing change in very marked fashion. The ironstone hills of the north drop steeply into Warwickshire and Gloucestershire. They are succeeded to the south by the clays and gravels of the Thames valley, which spread westwards over the Vale of the White Horse into Wiltshire and eastwards over the extensive marsh of Otmoor into the Vale of Aylesbury. The present southern boundary is formed by the chalk and flint hills of the Downs and the Chilterns.

The pattern of settlement has been influenced by the river valleys, which also determined the lay-out of the two historic counties. Pre-conquest Oxfordshire lay to the north of the river Thames, the frontier of the old kingdom of Wessex within which, to the south, lay Berkshire. Here, the Vale of the White Horse was almost bisected by the river Ock, fed by various small streams, and crossed also by the Ginge or Mill Brook flowing northwards from the slopes of the Downs. Oxfordshire was divided north-south by the deep valley of the river Cherwell, fed by the river Ray from the east and by the Sor brook and the river Swere from the west. At Oxford, Cherwell and Thames joined; a further tributary, the Thame, entered downstream. Upstream tributaries are the Glyme and the Dorn, the Evenlode and the Windrush. Each of these river valleys has its own character, separated from its neighbour by steep-sided hills. At the watershed of three rivers, one flowing westwards out of the county, one east into the Cherwell and a third south into the Thames stands Chipping Norton.

Oxford itself came into existence only in the eighth century AD, as the site chosen as a place of refuge by a Saxon princess seeking to escape an unwanted marriage. It later became useful to the armies of Wessex as an outpost fort in the tenth-century struggle to prevent the Danes penetrating further south than the river Thames when the city's first fortifications were built.

Oxford remained an urban settlement in isolation; its history is atypical, partly because in the twelfth century it became a university town. Its denizens found their livelihood from its transient population; bequests and endowments to colleges made possible a continuous building programme commanding some of the most able talent in the world. The university, a law unto itself, was a law unto the city also, since for centuries the university officers held a jurisdiction which elsewhere belonged to the local lord.

While the townsmen of Oxford were losing their pre-eminence the smaller settlements were growing in size. Their advantage was often water power – undoubtedly one of the county's most important assets and it is in the river valleys that the region's settlements are the thickest, their inhabitants supported by a mixture of agricultural and industrial pursuits. Water was essential to power mills and for the fulling and dyeing of cloth. The concentration of mills is revealed in the Domesday survey of 1086 and, surprisingly little changed, in the detailed maps of Rocque and Davis in the eighteenth century. Mills often changed function and survive amongst the county's most permanent monuments, even if heavily restored. For as long as wood was the only alternative fuel, water power remained important, made redundant only when the Industrial Revolution created a manufacturing base further north.

It is a paradox of the region that while its natural focus might appear to be the river Thames, in fact much of the region's history lies well away from its largest river's meandering course. The Thames has a very gradual fall between Lechlade and Henley – only some 175 feet (53.34 m) in 75 miles (46 kms). Upstream from Oxford, settlement stayed at a prudent distance from the banks. The river, slow flowing, lacked the capacity to power mills without the construction of special mill streams; these, when constructed, hindered navigation. The river was very shallow and, worst of all, it flooded regularly. So although prehistoric man's settlements are found on the gravel terraces between Dorchester and Stanton Harcourt, and a string of Saxon place names suggests that at least some invaders approached by river, the waters of the Thames were man's doubtful ally.

The bridging of the Thames is the history of the region in miniature. Only one of the many fords by which the river was once crossed is still clearly visible, that at Duxford. The oldest bridge is at Radcot, mentioned first in 995 and later rebuilt. Until 1250, when Newbridge, some eight miles downstream, was erected, Radcot was the only bridge before Oxford and then Abingdon. The rebuilding of this bridge, together with the construction of a new bridge at Culham crossing the abbot of Abingdon's canal around 1415, represented the last efforts until the eighteenth-century turnpike roads brought Tadpole, Swinford and Shillingford bridges into existence. In the nineteenth century the railway too had to cross the Thames – at Kennington, Nuneham, Appleford and, thanks to Isambard Kingdom

Brunel, at Moulsford. Other nineteenth-century structures include Clifton Hampden, Sutton Courtenay and the Oxford Gas Coal and Coke Company bridge. Donnington Bridge, opened in 1962, forms part of Oxford's defences against the motor car.

Arthur Young, in spite of his comments, knew that the wealth of the area lay in its agriculture. It was already rich by the time of the Domesday survey; twenty-five years before the Black Death struck in 1348 it was the wealthiest area in England. This wealth has been consistently maintained, the explanation for the enormous number, and variety, of buildings from the middle ages to the late eighteenth century. The area was sheltered from the dramatic effects of the Industrial Revolution, for it offered no ports, few mineral resources, and only indifferent connections by either road or water. Turnpike roads and two canals brought in cheaper manufactured goods and cheaper coal, providing the impetus to establish a number of small ironworks. The new roads also made it easier to transport perishable foodstuffs to London. Later, a network of railways did far more to change the balance, bringing nearer the steadily growing influence of the metropolis. The railway did not only supersede transport by road and water from a fertile hinterland; it spewed people outwards. By the end of the nineteenth century trains brought about the building of comfortable villas at Henley and Goring amd small country seats in the Bicester area. In the course of the century many of the small towns experienced a sudden spurt of life and were decorated with large municipal buildings – not just town halls but police stations, workhouses, hospitals and schools. But they were still self-sufficient communities, market centres for a county which, despite the depression in farming, was until 1918 predominantly agricultural.

The First World War brought the first of the airfields, but it was the after-effects of the war that really brought substantial change, in particular the loss of manpower in the villages and the establishment in Oxford of the factories belonging to William Morris, manufacturer of the Bull-nosed Cowley and the Morris Minor. The city of Oxford spread far beyond its medieval walls and for a short time was turned into an industrial town. Within thirty years the villages of Cowley, Headington, Marston, Summertown, Wolvercote, Binsey and Littlemore were all absorbed within the city's boundaries.

The twentieth century has seen other industrial developments – Northern Aluminium came to Banbury in 1931. The Second World War brought more airfields. In addition to the establishment of light engineering industries, post-war developments include the establishment of AERE at Harwell, the European JET/TORUS project at Culham and the building of

8

the power station at Didcot – perhaps Oxfordshire's most dramatic monument and certainly its most inescapable. These undertakings have all marked the landscape; they have also brought new people, demanded more housing and injected new money.

It is ironic that the county's newest road should return the county town to its traditional isolation. The M40, completed in 1989-90, slices across the northeast of the area on a line as unhistorical as the revised boundaries of the county itself. To traverse its forty-two miles provides a quick glimpse of every period since man first occupied the region. To turn off it is far more rewarding. This book is written for those who go in search of the fascination of Oxfordshire's history, as well as its beauty.

A note on terminology
The unification of two historic counties on which all administration was based between 1086 and 1974 creates a problem for the historian. To overcome repetitious explanation, the phrase 'the Vale' refers to that part of Berkshire added to historic Oxfordshire to make the modern county of that name, while the word Oxfordshire refers specifically to the pre-1974 county. The distinction has been maintained in chapters after the Norman Conquest. The words the area, the region or the county mean the modern unit.

Money Values
It is almost impossible to give sensible modern money equivalents for the system of reckoning in pounds (£), shillings (s.) and pence (d.) or pennies used in this country until 1971. One simple way is for the reader to think in terms of modern values. Twelve pennies made a shilling, twenty shillings made a pound. A mark was 13s.8d., a guinea twenty-one shillings.

Prehistoric Peoples

Prehistoric man has left two impressive monuments in the area later to become Oxfordshire – on the Downs at Wayland's Smithy and at Rollright, on the ridge on the northwest edge of the county. Wayland's Smithy is a chambered long barrow covering two separate multiple burials of different dates. The earlier barrow capped a wooden structure built over a sarsen pavement, with a chalk revetment from quarry ditches along each side; this was subsequently covered by the long trapezoidal mound, 180 feet (54 m), fronted by the fine sarsen forecourt and burial chambers seen today. Radio-carbon provides a date of around 2820 BC. The skeletons of twenty-two people were found here, but how they lived we do not know.

The Whispering Knights at Rollright is the oldest of a group of long barrows found on the Cotswold slopes southwards to the river Thames. The four uprights and a slipped capstone mark the site of a burial, all of which were on the same pattern. The now isolated sarsen stone, the most common survival, was the upright which closed the entrance to a chambered mound in which the body, along with possessions, was placed. Other such stones are to be seen at Spelsbury, Langley, Steeple Aston and, at Enstone, the Hoar Stone which gave its name to the village. Much more of what was built, still visible to those recording boundaries of Saxon estates in the tenth century AD, has long since gone. At Ascott under Wychwood the barrow has been excavated. The bones of forty-seven people, buried in a series of separate cells, were recovered, ranging in age from less than a year old to fifty. The adults were between 5'2" (1.57 m) and 5'4" (1.62m) tall and many of them had died in their twenties. It probably took about 7,000 manhours to build the covering mound. Reconstructed in the County Museum at Woodstock, this barrow, if typical, must, together with the others on the slopes of the Evenlode valley, represent a centre of local power and considerable wealth.

Neolithic peoples also were probably the builders of the stone circle called the King's Men at Rollright. Some seventy of the original one hundred and five stones remain, placed in a circle with only a single, narrow opening, their purpose ceremonial rather than funeral. It is difficult now to understand that this rivalled Stonehenge and Avebury, the only two larger circles in England, but perhaps easier to comprehend the fascination it exercised for Tudor antiquaries as it does for present day archaeologists. An equally splendid circle, the Devil's Quoits, its stones long since thrown to the ground, lay on the gravels at Stanton Harcourt. Damaged first by the runway of a temporary airfield and subsequently by gravel extraction it has shared the fate of much of the evidence from the prehistoric period.

The builders of these monuments were not the earliest inhabitants of the area, though they were the earliest to leave behind more than primitive flint tools and weapons. About 3000 BC changes in the landscape are observable. The Neolithic, or New Stone, Age, people had primitive ploughs and digging sticks with which to prepare the ground for wheat and barley. They possessed sickles for harvesting their crops which were stored in pits dug in the ground, and stones for grinding. They made pottery, some of it distinctively decorated. Animals were also kept, even though hunting was still important. To what extent these were a nomadic people and to what extent they enjoyed a settled existence is uncertain. A degree of communal organisation is suggested by the existence of ten causewayed camps, one of which has been excavated at Abingdon; they may have been commercial, political, religious and social centres. There is also evidence for an import trade – of stone axes from Cumbria, North Wales and Cornwall – and of more localised exchanges between the Cotswolds and the Downs where we have seen the most dramatic monuments.

From about 2000 BC evidence of Bronze Age settlers is widely found throughout the county, often on the same sites as their predecessors. Whether these settlements represent conquest by peoples coming from the continent or the adoption of the latest technology by the already settled population is not clear. The King's Stone, yet another monument to be seen at Rollright, is the upright marker stone for a Bronze Age cemetery sited on the northern side of the escarpment.

The concentration of monuments at Rollright, in association with surface finds from a wide area suggesting settlement, may perhaps be explained by the fact that the sites stand at a nodal point of some of the earliest hilltop trackways. We cannot say when such routes came into existence or for what purpose – the migration of peoples, the furtherance of trade or the driving of cattle. Neither can we be certain, in view of the increasing number of valley settlements now known to archaeologists, that they really were the main lines of communication they appear to be. Nevertheless, the lines of five such routes across Oxfordshire are very clear. From Rollright the route runs north to Banbury and beyond: it cuts south via Chipping Norton to Burford. At this point it splits, branching southwest out of the county and southeast towards Faringdon, Wantage and thereafter over the fairly clearly defined Icknield Way to the much broader Ridgeway. The Icknield Way and the Ridgeway themselves strike east-west across what is now the county's southern boundary, parallel to but some twenty miles south of another east-west route, the later Roman Akeman Street from Bicester to Burford and beyond. The fifth clear line, the Portway, ran from north to south along the high ground on the east side of the river Cherwell; it passed through later Oxford.

The Bronze Age settlers seem to have preferred the gravel terraces of the Thames valley to the wooded slopes further north where, though the shields found at Eynsham and Dorchester and the cauldron from Shipton on Cherwell on display in the Ashmolean Museum, are all fine pieces, Bronze Age finds are scant. Further south, however, there were monuments; one, Barrow Hills at Radley, has disappeared under a housing estate. A two acre (0.80 ha) enclosure, protected by a flat-bottomed ditch and an internal bank, later strengthened by a palisade, is visible at Rams Hill and some round barrows, nearly ploughed out, at Churn Down above Blewbury. Agricultural activities may be represented in the so-called 'Celtic Fields' to be seen on the Downs, called for by population increase.

Around 800 BC came new ideas and revolutionary technology. Iron, tougher and more durable, replaced the use of bronze as the stock material for implements. People then began to extract iron from the ironstone to be found in the north of the county; smelting pits have been discovered at Church Hanborough. Iron currency bars were buried within Madmarston hill fort, the characteristic monument of this period and amongst the best examples in the area. The term 'fort' is perhaps too grandiose. While their construction represents a significant increase of communal effort and may reflect greater resources of manpower, it is not certain that these places were constructed against threat of attack or were associated with warfare. Certainly defensible, they more probably served as points for the exchange of goods for, alongside the northern trackways, lie the 'forts' of Chastleton, North Newington, Tadmarton, Ilbury, Idbury and Lyneham.

Even more impressive examples are to be seen on or near the Ridgeway. Blewburton Hill, which already had a four acre (1.61 ha) Bronze Age enclosure, was refortified in the fifth-fourth centuries BC with a V-shaped ditch to enclose a larger area; it was further defended by a timber-laced rampart. In the mid-fourth century a village of small circular timber houses was erected. Segsbury Hill boasted a very large enclosure, of twenty-six and a half acres (10.72 ha) within a single ditch and rampart, erected at this period. Some earlier sites were reused; Ram's Hill was refortified to enclose seven acres (2.83 ha), but was occupied only briefly in the sixth and fifth centuries before being abandoned, possibly in favour of the more defensible site high above it at Uffington, easily the most impressive today.

Uffington's eight acres (3.23 ha) were protected by a single ditch and rampart laced with timber and revetted by sarsen stones. Below it was cut the famous White Horse, whether by the Iron Age peoples, as similar horses on their coins would suggest, or earlier by their Bronze Age predecessors as scientific dating would have us believe, we do not know. Measuring some 365 feet (111.3 m), it was easily seen, but we can only guess at its purpose; it may have been intended to claim territory, or to mark a meeting place or market.

Last in line is the two acre (0.80 ha) Alfred's Castle in Ashdown Park; its single rampart, revetted by sarsen stones, is still clearly visible.

By the beginning of the first century BC, when Oxfordshire was a frontier zone, a network of forts covered the Vale. The site at Blewburton was strengthened yet again around 100 BC. It commands a wide view of the Vale, in particular of Sinodun Camp on Wittenham Clumps, a landmark for miles around, which protected the long occupied Dyke Hills on the other side of the Thames. It would surely have been possible to signal from Blewburton to all the camps in the area, those on the Downs and the three on the heavy clays of the Vale; unexcavated Badbury, a nine acre (3.64 ha) fort between Faringdon and Coleshill, Furze Hill above Little Coxwell, a square fort of twelve acres (4.85 ha), both lying close to a track running southeast-northwest, and finally to Cherbury. Cherbury, though slightly higher than the surrounding marshland, is the only fort not on high ground. It has three close-set banks and ditches enclosing nine acres (3.64 ha), entered through a metalled causeway at the northeast. It is one of the latest forts in the area, dated to the first half of the first century AD, the years just before the Roman invasion.

By then the settlers south of the Thames, the Atrebates, were under pressure from the Dobunni to the west and the Catuvellauni to the east. The Catuvellauni, under their king Cunobelin, Shakespeare's Cymbeline, spread their influence, not always by peaceful means, over much of the region's eastern parts. Earthworks of this period, all known as Grim's Ditch, lie between the rivers Windrush and Glyme near Ditchley and on the Downs parallel with but just below the Ridgeway. Other sections of similar bank and ditch can be seen in three other places; further west at Knighton, north of Oxford in Aves Ditch above the Cherwell and to the east above Mongewell running up the slope of the Chilterns. Various interpretations have been given to these earthworks; those near Ditchley are possibly defensive, while the Mongewell section, also pre-Roman, is interpreted as a boundary between two differing settlement patterns, an earlier one on light soils cultivated and used for sheep-rearing, the second and later based on pig and cattle farming.

Details of the coming of the Romans are unknown. Their arrival does not seem to have been particularly violent. Some of the inhabitants of Blewburton died in battle; collapsed ramparts, buried animals and a burned gateway suggest an attack, but whether by a hostile neighbouring tribe or the Romans is not known. This site was deserted thereafter; elsewhere the Romans seem to have spared the settlements. For example, an Iron Age village which had existed at Frilford Heath from about 350 BC is represented by pits, ditches and occupation debris; a second settlement dates to around 150 BC. To its huts and cooking pits was added a substantial timber building enclosed by a ditch. It probably had a religious function because the Romans took over the site, constructing a temple with a rotunda over the earlier building, a practice common in the early years of the Roman conquest as part of the effort to colonise the country.

The Romans

The new conquerors, in some haste to subdue their new territory, saw no need to establish a major governmental or military town in Oxfordshire, possibly because there was no large tribal capital and no sizeable population. Nothing is known about the nature or the course of the conquest, nor can any guess be made as to why the newcomers' administrative arrangements appear to have ignored the area. Nevertheless, despite the absence of large settlements, the region lost its peripheral relationship to surrounding areas through the development of a road system rather different from that which had served earlier needs. The focal points of this system, all of which lay outside our boundaries, enclosed the Oxfordshire region. The civilian towns of Verulamium (St Albans) and Towcester and the garrison towns of Cirencester and Silchester, were the centres of importance; the rich agricultural land of Oxfordshire supplied their food and clothing requirements.

Two major Roman roads bisect the area. The north-south line left the Watling Street near Towcester, entering the county at Finmere. Represented today by the A421, it passed through the newly founded military depot of Alchester and continued southwest across Otmoor. Stumps of four timber piles to carry a bridge over the river Ray have been discovered at Ivy Farm, Fencott. The road continued over Shotover Hill to Dorchester, the second base established by the Romans as a small military camp. Though traced in only a short section, the line appears to have continued southwards on the west side of the Thames, passing through Aston Tirrold, towards Silchester.

The second road, now known as the Akeman Street, possibly followed an earlier prehistoric trackway. It connected St Albans with Cirencester, entering the county near Blackthorn, passing through Alchester and continuing west in a straight line to cross the Cherwell near Kirtlington. Marked now by footpaths, it traversed Blenheim Park, and then successively crossed the rivers Glyme, Evenlode and Windrush before leaving the county beyond Holwell.

Other roads, now less easily traceable and possibly less important, also existed. One, known later as the Portway, ran southeast from Somerton to Kirtlington, where it joined the Akeman Street; part of its line is marked by the modern road connecting Upper Heyford and Kirtlington. There may have been a southern continuation to the Thames crossing at Oxford. There was certainly a continuation over Boar's Hill to Frilford, after which its route is the present A338 to Wantage; here its line was used in Saxon times to mark the parish boundary. It left the county over the Downs. Two others originated on the Fosse Way, the route between Cirencester and Lincoln. One led to Chipping Norton, the other entered the county near Epwell to run southeast to Madmarston, Swalcliffe Lea and Tadmarton, there to split. One branch ran eastwards, probably via Broughton and Bodicote and out of the county near King's Sutton, heading for Towcester; the other continued southeast past Great Tew, Wootton and so to the line of the Akeman Street. South of the Thames the Icknield Way almost certainly continued in use, though, unlike the others, it does not seem ever to have been metalled.

Along, or within easy reach of, these metalled roads villa farms developed. On them the economic life of the region focused, much stimulated by the markets and the needs of the new military centres. The shift of settlement away from the gravel terraces to the heavier, but far more productive, soils of the western uplands is very marked. Settlements on the Banbury Redlands and the now apparently isolated sites at Great Tew and Steeple Aston, only some five miles north of the Akeman Street, suggest a fairly heavily exploited agricultural belt. The thickest concentration of villas, however, lay near the points where this road crossed the Glyme, Evenlode and Windrush, while another group was sited along the springline of the Downs near the Icknield Way, at Lewknor, Letcombe Regis, West Challow, Kingston Lisle and Woolstone.

Many of these villas have been excavated, some more scientifically than others. At Woolstone exploration revealed a large farmstead, with an impressive mosaic pavement in its main living room. Its history was similar to that of one of the two villas in Ditchley Park. Here the house faced south onto a courtyard more than three hundred feet (91 m) square, enclosed first by a bank and ditch and later by a stone wall, presumably for the protection of both men and beasts. Beyond lay gardens and an orchard. The house was rebuilt four times; it developed from an oblong timber-framed rectangle with wattle and daub walls to an eight-roomed E-shaped colonnaded house built in stone with a tiled roof. Its latest and largest granary could store the produce from a thousand acres (404 ha).

Ditchley was not amongst the grandest. The last phase of North Leigh shows that in the fourth century it had become the square courtyard house that can be visited today. Facing southeast in a sheltered spot on the banks of the Evenlode, the chief living rooms on the northwest and northeast looked out over the river, with baths on the north and east sides. A heated room formed the western corner, presumably for use in winter, in which the surviving mosaic can still be seen. The other wing contained workshops and stables. Internally the rooms were connected by a colonnade facing onto an enormous courtyard, occupying some three-quarters of an acre (0.30 ha). Beyond large and numerous outbuildings was a garden. Early excavations, in 1783 and 1815-16, made it difficult for the third, in 1908, to establish the plans of the earlier houses, but in all probability North Leigh's history was similar to that of Ditchley; a period of desolation in the third century, followed by revival in the fourth and habitation in part, though not all, of the structure at the beginning of the fifth.

Other villa sites are known in the Evenlode valley; one each at Wilcote and Stonesfield, two at Fawler. Three others lay in the Windrush valley at Little Minster, Asthall and at Widford, where a mosaic floor lies beneath the small church. The word Fawler, also found in the Vale, denotes a 'floor', though none survives in the villages whose names remind us of their existence. Other examples, from Stonesfield, were of a quality that suggests they may have been constructed by the mosaicists working from the major town of Cirencester. One, discovered in 1712, depicted Bacchus and a panther; it was destroyed by the losing party in a wrangle over sharing the profits from its public display. Others, with geometrical, patterns, found at Great Tew and Steeple Aston, now lost, were drawn by a seventeenth century antiquarian.

Although Roman Oxfordshire may disappoint visually, a picture of very considerable wealth emerges from the fragmented or ruined finds. In addition to agriculture, there was one major industry, important also beyond the region's bounds. Pottery was made in a chain of kilns on the hills above Oxford, stretching from later Headington and Cowley to Sandford on Thames, an area where clay and wood to fire the kilns co-existed. Wares made here, ranging from coarse kitchen vessels to the finest table vessels with painted decoration, flagons and late imitations of imported plates and bowls, have been found as far away as London, probably transported there by river.

Neither known town was large. Alchester, at the junction of the Akeman Street and the Towcester-Silchester road, only ever enclosed twenty-five acres (10.12 ha) within its ramparts; it probably replaced a temporary camp at nearby Little Chesterton, but it was never more than a posting station and store depot. Dorchester, at a river crossing and the confluence of Thames and Thame, was even smaller, never exceeding twelve and a half acres (5.06 ha), though it had acquired stone defences and a massive temple by the first century AD. An altar to Jove erected here by Marcus Vatrius Severus named the region's only known Roman inhabitant; it is now lost.

The large number of chance Roman finds at Wallingford and Abingdon makes it possible that there were small settlements by the river crossings; other, apparently later, town sites may also have had Roman origins. A large sprawling settlement of fifty acres (20.24 ha) existed at Swalcliffe in the north of the county, where the road pattern suggests that this part of the county was not so isolated at this period as it later became.

Two, possibly three, sites of earlier importance continued in use throughout the period; Woodeaton, Frilford and Lowbury Hill. Here, above Blewbury and just north of the Ridgeway, a square rectangular earthwork marks the site of a small temple. At Woodeaton a temple had been built before the end of the first century AD. At Frilford there was extensive building activity at the close of the fourth century: a second temple was built, a cemetery established across the road from it, the street system extended and an amphitheatre constructed. Occupation debris suggests the existence of something approaching a small town. By the fifth century though the temple was less frequented, the cemetery, like many of the villas scattered through the county, was still in use, despite the collapse of Roman rule after the withdrawal of the legions to protect more central areas of the empire under threat from the Germanic invasions.

Saxon Settlement

The best place from which to view the beginnings of Anglo-Saxon Oxfordshire is the large barrow on the ridge south of Asthall village where the A40 joins the B4047. A clearly visible landmark, the tree-capped mound stands out, an obvious viewpoint from which the man buried below might well have surveyed his kingdom stretching over the flat lands of the upper Thames and Windrush valleys. The mound covers the ashes of a man sent to the afterlife with his horse and a selection of goods which include an elaborate suite of strap-fittings, a cast metal bowl in a Byzantine style, an antique silver cup, horn or perhaps wooden vessels which had decorated metal mounts, continental pottery and a board game with bone counters. It is the only burial in England other than Sutton Hoo to have yielded a solid silver vessel; the goods buried with him declare a man of both wealth and status.

He remains nameless and unidentified; the style of the burial and the date of the vessels suggest that he was one of the last pagans, possibly an incomer from the Anglian kingdom of Mercia. By the time of his death, some two hundred and fifty years after the withdrawal of the Roman legions, the first confused period of England's infiltration by the Germanic tribes of Angles, Saxons and, in Kent, Jutes, was over.

The arrival of Angles and Saxons in Oxfordshire is hard to chart, even using all the sources – documentary, archaeological, topographical, place names. It may well be that the reality was indeed as confused as the picture painted by scholars. For the two centuries which preceded the Asthall burial we know for certain only that Germanic settlement pockmarked the Thames valley within a hundred years of the withdrawal of the legions, in 410 AD. A few people, like the mercenary soldier buried at Dorchester, may have been inveigled into staying, his military skills welcomed against his own people. Others simply came and conquered. Some sailed up the river Thames, each leader staking out his own territory, each settlement a little higher upstream, all containing the Saxon *-ingas* suffix denoting territory controlled by one tribe; Sonning, Reading, Goring, Shillingford, Bensington (now Benson), Wallingford and Abingdon, with outposts at Cassington, Kirtlington, Faringdon, Uffington and Watlington. These sites have similar topographical features. They were always on gravel banks just slightly higher than the surrounding countryside, no longer always notice-able but clearly visible at one such settlement, Chimney (Ceomma's island), on the banks of the Thames above Swinford Bridge.

The Thames was not the only route by which the invaders penetrated. Others may have come from East Anglia, travelling along the Icknield Way; the line of hamlets spaced at intervals so regular from east to west suggests the same deliberate pattern of settlement found along the Thames. Each village lay at the centre of a block of land, delineated as the later parish. One, Blewbury, to the east of the river crossing at Wallingford, is several times the size of the others. A similar pattern of rectangular parish shapes can be observed either side of the river Cherwell where the river was used as the base line. All these groups steered carefully clear of the Chilterns, which seem to have been the territory of yet another people.

In a few cases the villas on the line of the Akeman Street continued in use, at least for as long as the buildings remained in good condition. When they started to become ruinous, their new inhabitants abandoned rather than repaired them, presumably because they lacked the necessary skills. We know more of the burial customs of the new settlers than of their living conditions. Their evidence shows us a warlike society, the high ranking men the owners of spears and shields, their womenfolk the possessors of abundant high quality jewellery, the lower class engaged in rather primitive farming to supply barley, oats, milk and meat; woodland and waste were important for feeding pigs and cattle, pasture for sheep. Skins from the animals had many uses: weaving is much in evidence. Houses were built by sinking posts into the ground and filling the spaces with wattle and daub. Settlement sites were rarely compact, but sprawled over large areas as buildings needed replacement. Religion stressed the placating of spirits, some of whose names are revealed in place names.

In 571 battles were fought at Eynsham and Benson by a chieftain named Cuthwulf and in 584 another at Stoke Lyne by his relatives, Cutha and Ceawlin. A barrow at Cuddesdon excavated in 1847, now ploughed out, has tentatively been associated with a chieftain of Ceawlin's dynasty, the Gewissae, because the name derives from Cutha's dun. The finds included two swords, two Kentish blue glass bowls (on display in the Ashmolean Museum), a bronze bucket probably from the eastern Mediterranean and a garnet-studded bronze fragment. Laid radially round the barrow were several skeletons, all of them lying face down, their heads away from the barrow and their legs crossed. In all probability these were victims whose sacrifice accompanied the burial of the exceptionally important. To what extent the military events reflected political change is unknown. What is clear is that the people who held sway between 570 and 630 had more so-phisticated taste than their predecessors. They introduced different customs; these included the practice of burial in older barrows with exotic jewellery similar to that found at the contemporary Frankish court, the reuse of Roman villas as dwelling places and, for their leaders only, the construction of large timber halls, one of which has been excavated at Drayton near Abingdon.

An even bigger change was soon to take place. Up to this time we have been looking at a pagan society. In the late 630s Cynegils, ruler in the Dorchester area, entertained a Christian missionary, Birinus, sent by pope Honorius I to convert the peoples of middle England. How far Cynegils was a true believer, and to what extent it had become politic, possibly even inevitable, to be converted to a faith to which many of his contemporaries subscribed, cannot be known.

Bede, author of the *Ecclesiastical History of the English Peoples*, the period's most detailed and reliable source, tells us that Birinus 'built and dedicated several churches and brought many people to God'. One preaching spot where he is supposed to have addressed the crowds is identified at Churn Knob above Blewbury. The location is not implausible – on a royal estate and within view of both the royal vill at Benson and of the Roman city of Dorchester, given to Birinus as the seat of his bishopric.

The progress of Christianity was at the mercy of personalities. Oxfordshire plunged again into chaos when Cynegil's son, Cenwalh, repudiated his wife, daughter of the ambitious, expansionist and unconverted Penda, king of Mercia, the present West Midlands. A marriage contracted no doubt for the protection of an Oxfordshire kingdom turned sour; attacked by his father-in-law, Cenwalh withdrew southwards to Winchester, thus ensuring his survival and the safety of the dynasty which was later to rule all England. Oxfordshire in the meantime passed under the control of the Mercian kings and remained under their influence for the next one hundred and fifty years.

To this period belong a scatter of large round barrows, each occupying prominent sites in northwest Oxfordshire. One is the barrow at Asthall, already discussed, another the rather smaller, and unexcavated, example at Lew, not far from a cluster of cemeteries on the lower reaches of the river Windrush below Witney. Finds from all the cemetery sites reveal objects in a style differing from that known to be earlier; many of these objects are Anglian in style, not Saxon. Once again traces of a change in society, from the Saxon Gewissae to the Mercian Angles, may be preserved in burials. The custom of grave goods was reserved for the few and was no longer universal. The church was beginning to exert its influence – in more than one way. Increasingly, it is documentary evidence, emanating from the churchmen, that allows us to reconstruct events. After the initial shock of the Mercian invasion a stable peace saw the development of the area.

The character of society was changing. One man, a king, was coming to rule ever larger territory; small, probably tribal, power bases were amalgamated into provinces visited by an itinerant king and his retinue. They had to be fed and housed. It is from this period that we first read of the *villae regales*, royal villages. One was Blewbury, the largest of the Icknield Way settlements. Others were Faringdon, Wantage, Abingdon, Benson, Headington, Bampton, Bloxham, Kirtlington and Wootton. In all these the king was the chief, perhaps the sole, landowner. Blewbury is of special interest since in 944 king Edmund gave to bishop Aelfric 1000 *mensae* of land, which Aelfric then presented to Abingdon Abbey. Its boundaries were described in a charter, enough of whose landmarks can be identified to suggest that the area was that now contained within the parish boundaries of Aston Tirrold, Aston Upthorpe and North and South Moreton. Blewbury, as described one hundred and forty-five years later in Domesday Book, was a place of about four hundred people with four mills and a church; the greatest landowner was still the king.

By 800 the Oxfordshire landscape was thick with minster churches, served by a group of clergy sharing a communal life. Their true origins are lost in legends constructed by the devotion of later hagiographers. They were, however, clearly erected to the memory of some local charismatic figure, male or female, and developed and endowed on a generous scale by kings, princes and governors – at Shipton under Wychwood, Charlbury, Bampton, Thame, Oxford, Eynsham, Abingdon and Bicester; all except Shipton later developed into important towns. These communities, tied to the liturgical round, did not always have the time to make themselves entirely self-sufficient; neither did they need to be, for the lands and estates which were given to them made it possible for them to live off their estates. Surplus in one year might add to cash in hand; slowly the selling of what was not needed and the buying of what could not be obtained locally stimulated economic development. Round the minsters congregated the merchants; gradually the minster sites became the foci for market activities and for urban growth.

Monasteries, groups of men or women sharing a communal life, succeeded minster sites in these functions in a still under-populated countryside. The most significant of them is perhaps the nunnery established by the princess Frideswide. At some time in the eighth century, Frideswide, seeking to escape an unwanted marriage, took refuge among the marshes of what was later to be Oxford. Excavation has shown that the streets of the town, smaller than the later city, were laid out on a grid plan by the mid-ninth century. The north-south axis was the present Cornmarket, the east-west Queen Street and the High. The streets were lined with timber houses and small shops. By the time written records mention Oxford the town was already old. Its defences, erected in the early tenth century by king Edward the Elder, their length and the duties of maintenance laid out in a document called the Burghal Hidage, added to Oxford's prestige. The fact that it was the only fort in a comprehensive scheme of fortification against the Danes to be erected on the north bank of the Thames marks it out as already being a place of importance.

The sections of ditch and bank raised at Wallingford are nowadays far more impressive and much easier to appreciate than the Saxon remains of Oxford. Another of the deliberately created towns, Wallingford's present street plan is essentially that laid out in the tenth century. The south and west sections of the defences are best seen bounding the open spaces of Kinecroft and continuing west and north in Bullcroft Park almost to the later castle. The banks, some 2,115 yards (1934 m), are still, in the best preserved sections, 25 feet (7.62 m) high. On top of the bank stood a timber wall, so that any attacker would come under arrow fire as he tried to cross the wide ditch. Within the circuit streets were laid out on a grid plan, preserved today with only a few changes. The duties of maintenance and defence did not fall solely on the inhabitants; estates in the county were also deemed liable to provide a man at arms to defend a four to five foot section and were required also to assist in repair work.

These were belated measures of defence. From much earlier the Anglo-Saxon Chronicle makes frequent mention at least of the area's southern limits because they were ravaged by the new invaders, the Danes, who threatened the kingdom of Wessex for whose rulers the Chronicle was written. All through the ninth century, starting in 825, raids took place and were beaten off, with a greater or more often lesser degree of success, first by king Aethelwulf and then by his son, Alfred 'the Great' born at Wantage in 849. Following his defeat at Reading in 871, Alfred's retreat and pursuit to Ashdown and his victory there, supposedly at Alfred's Castle, was a turning point. Recovery began with a peace treaty, concluded in 878, which gave the Danes all the territory north of the Watling Street, some twenty miles from Oxfordshire's eastern boundary. The West Saxons kept everything to its south and west.

Threat of attack never entirely disappeared. Danish presence has been identified in Oxford itself and in a burial at Hook Norton. Innumerable swords have been found in the river Thames, almost certainly not all lost in battle and possibly thrown into the water during some ritual. Slowly the danger decreased until Danes could even be assimilated into the predominantly English population. Eventually it became safe enough even to reestablish the bishopric of Dorchester, incorporating land of the fugitive bishop of Leicester which included a large estate centred on Banbury. From 886 until 1072 lands from the Thames to the far distant Humber were in the care of the bishop of Dorchester.

In the tenth century written records begin to illuminate the scanty traces of the inhabitants. Grants of land with their detailed delineation of boundaries allow us to picture some areas in detail, for example the area round Witney, given to the bishop of Winchester in 969. The limits of this estate include the modern parishes of Curbridge, Crawley and Hailey. The northern part of the estate was heavily wooded. We read of thickets of hazel and willow; we walk from clearing to clearing – Nutley (where hazel nuts grow), Henley (the high clearing), Spoonley (the wood chipping clearing) and then pass down the huntsmen's way to the more open ground of the river's course. Here the landmarks are 'quaking marsh', 'slippery places' and 'foul island'. Charters preserve not only boundaries, some of them still those of today's parish, but also the contemporary landscape and the features of the past. The Blewbury charter of 944 for example mentions the Great Barrow, possibly the tumulus on Lowbury Hill, the Heathen Burial places at the Old Dyke, Fox Barrow, the Dyke of the Pointed Stone, the Sheepwashing place and the tall Cross at Heath Down, now Hadden Hill. The evidence of a large group of charters for contiguous areas of the Vale shows that land use was well organised. Crop land, meadow land and pasture were integral features of each estate and there seems to have been sufficient summer pasture for flocks and herds on the open downland above the cultivated fields. In the tenth century mills were established, often on the sites they would occupy continuously for centuries.

Prosperity was not confined to the Vale. At Oxford kings held at least four councils between 1015 and 1036. We also know of seven separate moneyers striking coins there in the century before the Conquest. Some of the communities flourishing on the Redlands in the north of the county were very wealthy indeed. Shipton under Wychwood, Hook Norton, Banbury and Deddington were all large places. Further south, Bampton and Abingdon, former *villae regales*, were each recorded in 1086 as having a market. Abingdon's community of merchants traded at the abbey gates, the abbey's wealth in some part generated from river traffic. Traders indeed successfully begged the abbot to excavate a canal between Abingdon and Culham which cut off the bend in the river and created Andersey island. From all who used the cut, the monks took a levy of one hundred eels from Candlemas to Easter, thus providing themselves with Lenten food. Their wealth soon after the Conquest can be pictured in a description of the actions of William's queen who decided to acquire some fine ornaments. She demanded that the monks bring their finest gifts; they brought their second best. Scorned by the disbelieving Matilda, they finally had to present her with the most magnificent – a chasuble with marvellous embroidery, a splendid choir cope, a white stole and a manuscript of the Gospels, covered with gold and gems in magnificent workmanship. Eynsham too was a market centre, no doubt stimulated by the presence of an abbey one of whose abbots, Aelfric, concerned himself with cultural pursuits.

Wealth there undoubtedly was, but physical remains of this period are few, probably because much was built of timber. Underneath the later castles at Middleton Stoney and Deddington archaeologists have uncovered the remains of a wooden Saxon hall; there must have been others. Buildings with ecclesiastical origins have fared little better. Indications of a Saxon church can be traced clearly at Bampton, North Leigh and Waterperry. At Caversfield there remains a double-splayed window halfway down the tower wall and at Swalcliffe deep slit windows above the eastern aisle arches. At Langford two crucifixion sculptures, one on the central tower and two others in the porch sides, are eloquent testimony to skills. It is probably no accident that the manor belonged to a noble and important landowner.

The most impressive example is the tower of St Michael at the Northgate in Oxford. It had three entrances; at ground level on the west face, at first floor level on the south side and, above the level of the defences on the second floor, in the north face. Above that was a two-stage belfrey with a pair of windows also facing outwards. It seems likely that the ground floor was used by officials on duty at the gate while the upper levels could be used for patrol or defence without either activity interrupting services being held within the church itself.

This, however, is an exceptional building, not just in the region but in England. Undoubtedly Oxfordshire had been wealthy for some time. Three outstanding pieces of jewellery, all to be seen in the Ashmolean Museum, reveal appreciation of beauty. The Sandford reliquary was small enough to be hung round the neck; it bears the figure of Christ in Majesty and has an inscription on the back. The Minster Lovell jewel and the Alfred jewel, both designed to be mounted on a short rod, both have flatbacked gold frames decorated with gold filigree; the inset consists of coloured glass set in panels between gold strips. The Alfred jewel shows a male figure holding two plants; the enamel is covered by a large piece of rock crystal. The Minster Lovell jewel, so called from the place of its finding, displays a simple cross. It is unlikely that any of these pieces was made in the county, but, together with the remaining fragmentary decoration of swords and architectural decoration, they provide our only glimpses of an elegant life style. The more perishable finery that would have decorated timber buildings is lost. Only coarse pottery is abundant, and even some of that was made outside the region.

The inadequate picture gained from existing finds cannot be accurate. Domesday Book, compiled in 1086, reveals the enormous prosperity which had made it possible to raise the Danegeld, the huge sums of gold required to buy off the Danes, and thus ensure a measure of safety. It also portrays a racially mixed society, consisting of landowners, great and small, entrepreneurs, moneyers, merchants and monks. Despite living with the ever present possibility of Danish raids, all were prospering in a prosperous area, engaged in the day to day business of securing their own future. Confirmation of a grant of land like the occasion when the widow Tova of Great Tew requested her neighbours from the nearby settlements to witness the transaction provide a glimpse of solidly wealthy landowners, their farms worked by peasants tied to the land. The monasteries, run on similar lines, received countless gifts, both of land and objects, another glimpse of the concerns of contemporaries.

The real monument to the Saxons is the creation of a society functioning within a well-defined administrative system. It was they who laid out the shire, or county, boundaries, over which they set the shire reeve or sheriff; the county was then divided into administrative units called the hundred, themselves subdivided by clerics into parishes. The county and the parish are still used as administrative units, though the hundred fell out of use in the sixteenth century. The codification of laws shows us clearly the involvement not only of the individual but also of the village in the structure of government. Just as lasting has been the pattern of settlement and the line of roads, nowadays often surviving just as lanes, that first came into being during these centuries.

It was the next wave of incomers who, inheriting an established settlement pattern and, aided and abetted by a number of fifth columnists, were both to change the area and to fix it in its present mould – the Normans.

From Norman Conquest to the Black Death
1066-1348

The new Norman overlords entered an already prosperous area, probably supporting a population of about 45,000, despite having enjoyed only one hundred and fifty years of peace. The main lines of communication between established settlements were in existence, the very extensive royal forests of Wychwood, Cornbury, Shotover and Stowood delimited. The landscape was already dotted with villages and with what can reasonably be called urban centres. Oxford and Wallingford had been created by the military needs of earlier generations, Abingdon and Eynsham as a result of settlement at the gates of an abbey, while Dorchester was the cathedral city for an area extending far beyond the county boundaries. Twenty years after his landing king William ordered a survey of his kingdom to be made and it is from this, Domesday Book, that we can construct a picture of the country he conquered.

Some of the most fertile land lay in the north beyond the river Swere. Here the Domesday survey recorded the highest concentration of plough teams and the highest density of population. There were two towns, Deddington being rather bigger than Banbury, a large number of villages and the greatest number of mills. Some villages already had three or more, driven by streams bordered by moderate amounts of meadow for grazing. Little woodland remained, a strong contrast to the area further south where the high ground was covered by Wychwood Forest, extending over some 50,000 acres (2024 ha) from Taynton east to Woodstock and from Ditchley south to Witney. Poorer soil supported far fewer people, though the river valleys sheltered many villages, some with extensive meadow land. Essential to provide a fresh supplement to meat and the 'fasting' food enjoined by the Church for consumption on Wednesdays and Fridays, every river had fisheries along the banks. Large numbers lay along the Cherwell; even more were concentrated on the Thames upstream from Dorchester and on the Ock.

Between this area and the Chilterns, the low-lying alluvial land of the Thames and the limestone hills of the Oxford Heights reveal extremes of prosperity. The claylands, centred on Dorchester, were amongst the most productive land, while marshy Otmoor, overlooked by the royal forests of Shotover and Stowood, was relatively poor. Meadowland along the streams was fairly abundant, but mills were few.

To the south, below the tree-covered Chilterns and the summits of the Downs, villages were sited along the springline, at the centre of land offering more grazing than arable. Trees thinned out on the chalk slopes of the Downs, but on either side of the Thames the same pattern of estates straddling different types of agricultural land was to be seen. Population density was at its highest, ranging from eleven to eighteen people per square mile. Many settlements were without mills though some, mostly along the Mill Brook and the chalk springline, had three. Large amounts of meadow made the area a centre of cheese production.

In the Vale the essential village pattern was already in existence. There were eighteen more villages in 1086 than there are today; no new villages were ever established. In Oxfordshire, already with at least two hundred and fifty-one separate settlements, many new ones were founded. Villages were small places; Seacourt, on the outskirts of Oxford where the western bypass now runs, had an adult male population of 27, in all perhaps 121 people. Cumnor, with 133 males, may have had a total of 465 inhabitants. Overall, Domesday Book, the record of both landholders and taxable wealth, reveals a picture of prosperity inherited in 1066 and already increasing only twenty years later, when the Book was written.

The record of land ownership is at least as interesting as the picture of land use. One hundred and twenty of William's followers were rewarded with land in the area, some receiving multiple grants. The king's half-brother, Odo bishop of Bayeux, for example, was given fifty-five manors, though this represents only 13% of his total estates in England. Robert d'Oilli, appointed sheriff, received almost as many. One of Odo's knights, Wadard, sufficiently influential to be embroidered into the needlework record of the Conquest, the Bayeux tapestry, was awarded Cogges, then on the main road to Oxford from Witney, where he took possession of his predecessor's timber hall beside a stone-built church.

The new Norman landholders worked hard and fast to consolidate their hold over the rich area they had acquired, beginning almost immediately to make their presence visible. A castle, with a large mound dominating an enclosed courtyard, was added to the existing defences of both Oxford and Wallingford. That at Wallingford guarded the Thames river crossing and was finished by 1071. That at Oxford was erected even more quickly, completed within two years of William's landing, even though it required the demolition of 480 houses. D'Oilli also built two bridges, the east or

Magdalen bridge and the south, Folly bridge, with its causeway the line of the present Abingdon Road, to connect into routes that would attract trade to the town and fill his coffers.

Other castles were built, probably by the 1090s, at Deddington, Swerford and Mixbury and, rather later, at Middleton Stoney, Ardley and Chipping Norton. Ascott under Wychwood, divided between two overlords, had the distinction of having also two castles. Most were constructed close to the church, where earthworks are still clearly to be seen at Chipping Norton, Middleton Stoney, Mixbury and Swerford. Later still, Hinton Waldrist and Faringdon were fortified, probably during the outbreak of fighting between rival claimants for the throne, Stephen and Matilda, beginning in 1138. Matilda's base was at Wallingford, three times besieged by Stephen. Peace was finally made there in 1153 and Matilda's son, Henry II, held his first Great Council there in 1155.

With the return of more peaceful conditions the less powerful, or the less well endowed, also began to build, though on a smaller scale and clearly with more than half an eye to their own physical comfort in the provision of a vaulted hall, sleeping quarters and decorated doorways. The Manor House at Appleton has a carved doorway. Norman Hall in Sutton Courtenay is a compact building on a rectangular plan, its hall at ground level, erected in 1191 by the lord of the manor. Sutton Courtenay 'Abbey', a building belonging to Abingdon Abbey, had a hall open to the rafters measuring around 36 feet in length and 21 feet wide (11 x 6.40 m).

The Normans influenced more than the appearance of towns and villages. They also altered the landscape by encouraging urban development. One such change occurred at Cogges around 1090 when the estate passed to a minor Norman family, the Arsics, whose ambition and improvements had radical effects on the countryside for centuries thereafter. First Manasses Arsic I gave the old manor house to the abbey of Fecamp in Normandy. A few of its monks took up residence, thus conferring status on the family as the possessors of a 'private' monastery. Their memory is preserved in the name Priory Farm, their monument is the church, far more splendid than might be expected in a village which at most boasted fifty inhabitants.

These buildings were dominated by Manasses' new residence on a site close to the Windrush southwest of the church. It is represented now by a pair of large, circular moated enclosures within which stood his 'castle', so massive that it was still remembered in the seventeenth century. It was a clear demonstration of the dual purposes of building; an imposing residence was both a statement of power and acted as a centre for the administration of scattered estates or manors.

For roughly one hundred years the Arsics were content to overlook the village which lay south of what is now Oxfordshire County Council's Farm Museum, where traces of earthworks and parallel ditches mark the site of its houses; its thirteenth and fourteenth century inhabitants are known from documents. But a mere village owing customary labour services to the lord's lands did not satisfy Robert Arsic, great grandson of the priory's founder. Like others, he sought to establish a town and to this end in 1212/13 he issued a charter to twenty-six people dividing up forty acres (16 ha) of his land between them. In return they were not only to pay him rent, but to build their own house on each plot. This is the nucleus of the settlement at Newland on the old A40 on the northeastern fringe of Cogges. Newland did not prosper; only seven of the original twenty-six rents could be accounted for in 1279 and indeed many of the plots seem to have remained empty until the nineteenth century.

Robert had no heir and the estate was divided between his two daughters. One continued to live in the castle, the other sold up. The new owners constructed a new house, the present Manor Farm which houses the Farm Museum.

Robert was in no way unique in his attempt to foster urban settlement. His neighbour at Witney, the bishop of Winchester, made two efforts, one before and another after Robert's attempt. Both were more successful. In 1206 he laid out new tenements on either side of the triangular green which extended away from the church and his palace and, in 1219/20, a second set of sixteen beyond the bridge over the Windrush. The development at Cogges had been hemmed in and outnumbered.

Whether Arsic and the bishop were in competition or collaboration is not known. They were both amongst the last to exploit their own lands in this way. Nearly a century before, on lands that had once been those of Odo of Bayeux at Burford, Robert Fitzhamon staked out plots running up the hill from the bridge over the Windrush, their frontages giving onto a broad street suitable for use as a market, in order the better to exploit the small settlement which lay on the fringe of his other estates. The same reasoning may lie behind the Fitzalans' decision to demarcate plots close to the castle in Chipping Norton. In 1135 the abbot of Eynsham laid out 'newlands', and a decade later the bishop of Lincoln enlarged Banbury and Thame by the layout of plots round a market place.

None of these experiments in urban creation represents a completely new town; they were all carefully controlled blocks of land grafted onto existing settlement and leased on terms which allowed the lessees greater control of their own fortunes than was permitted those who farmed lands for the benefit of the lord of the manor. Only the Crown established settlements on virgin land, at Woodstock and Henley. In 1279, when there was a nation-wide enquiry into the legitimacy of ancient rights, those called to give an account of Woodstock's liberties declared

> that Henry (II) often sojourned at Woodstock for love of a certain woman named Rosamund. At that time there was a certain waste place outside the said park and manor, and because the men of the said king were lodged too far from the manor house aforesaid, the Lord king with the unanimous assent and counsel of his nobles gave and granted divers parcels of land of the said waste place to divers men to build hostelries there for the use of the men of the same king. Also he established a market weekly on Tuesday, of which his bailiffs collected the toll, and that John established a three day fair at the feast of St Matthew.

It was Henry also who was said to 'have bought land in Henley for making buildings'. Exactly what he did is not known, but the regular boundaries of deliberately laid out plots are to be seen clearly on plans, their frontages giving onto the market place, their fortunes dependent on the entrepot river trade between London and the Thames valley hinterland.

The point behind this policy of enlarging existing settlements was not to benefit the existing town or its inhabitants but to swell the coffers of the overlord. The tolls on goods brought in for sale or to erect a stall, fines for short weight or poor quality together with the rents from properties made handsome profits from land which when farmed would have produced far less. The main feature of all these towns was a sizeable market place, most of them still quite easily seen today. At Henley it stretches uphill from the bridge over the Thames; at Burford uphill from the valley bridge; at Eynsham it is almost central, as it is at Witney where it occupied the green in front of the church. At both Banbury and Thame the extent of the original clear space has been concealed by later buildings.

Nevertheless, even in the early sixteenth century, the separate parts of Thame were apparent. The antiquary John Leland wrote that Thame was divided into three parts. 'Old Thame lies along the road from the church almost to the market place; New Thame consists of the market place and the finest part of the town in the direction of the London road. The third part is called Priest's End, the area round the church and the bridge towards Haseley'. One building remains, the Birdcage Inn, a three-storey fourteenth century structure which makes maximum use of a small ground plot to provide a shop and living quarters above, probably for a merchant. Both upper floors projected beyond the ground floor walls on three sides, giving the family extra room without requiring larger space.

Most of the enlarged towns prospered; in 1377 when the novel tax called the poll tax demanded a contribution of fourpence from every person over fourteen, we gain an approximate idea of size. 531 people paid in Banbury, 453 in Thame, 434 in Witney, 377 in Henley and 304 in Chipping Norton. Four years later a less reliable figure for Oxford shows that 2005 people were charged, but by then evasion was widespread and the inhabitants of Oxford may have been far more numerous. Eighty different trades were practised; they included 49 tailors, 29 brewers, 24 skinners, 23 weavers, 18 butchers, 16 bakers and 16 carpenters. There were also masons, slaters, locksmiths, tilers, coopers and ironmongers, together with two harp-makers, a chair-maker, a cap-maker and a garlic-monger. There were also some 1000 students, and it is their existence which makes Oxford's history very different from that of the other towns in the region.

In size Oxford might still be preeminent, but its economic superiority had long since waned. In the twelfth century Oxford had ranked high amongst English towns. Its commercially based wealth made it easy for the powerful Merchant Guild, made up of the most prosperous traders, to secure the grant of a charter in 1199, enabling it to elect its own officials – a mayor and bailiffs – instead of being governed by the king's sheriff. By then the city had reached the size it would retain for virtually six hundred years – from the Eastgate to the Castle and from St Michael at the Northgate to Christ Church. Around these points a new circuit of defences had been built by the early thirteenth century, surviving now in only one much rebuilt section in New College gardens. Outside the walls, only the foundation of four friaries and the Hospital of St John, now Magdalen College, increased the size of the medieval city.

Even by the start of the thirteenth century there is evidence that trade was already declining and that there were large numbers of empty properties. Part of the reason may have been the silting up of the river Thames so that it was no longer possible to transport goods either upstream or downstream. The city's tenuous links to a productive hinterland, able to supply the voracious demands of London, were broken, replaced around 1250 by a route crossing the Thames much higher upstream at Newbridge. This bridge carried trade from Burford and Witney to Abingdon, Dorchester and Henley without entering Oxford.

It was not all gloom. Oxford was far removed physically from the control of the bishop of Lincoln and this absence of ecclesiastical disapproval for new ideas, together with edicts prohibiting study abroad, may well have encouraged scholars to settle in a town still one of the most important in southern England. Teachers are known from the 1180s, and empty proper-

Above left: Wayland's Smithy

Above right: Asthall Barrow

Below left: St. Michael at the Northgate, Oxford

Below right: The font, Hook Norton Church

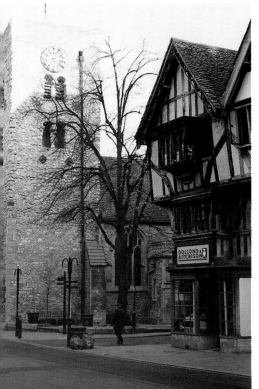

Left: Great Coxwell barn

Centre left: The Birdcage Inn, Thame

Centre right: Hanwell Castle

Below: Culham Bridge, Abingdon

ties were rented out by the townsfolk to small groups of teachers and students, the tentative beginnings of the collegiate system on which Oxford University still functions.

The interests of town and gown soon came into conflict. The influx of several hundreds of masters and students requiring lodging and food created problems of supply and even more of control. Clashes, brawls and even riots were frequent; whatever the cause, and whatever the justice of the situation, the University almost invariably won, eventually taking unto itself many of the administrative functions which had once belonged to the mayor and bailiffs. By the mid-fourteenth century, the town occupied a subordinate position, where it stayed for some five hundred years.

Trade and traders thus had good reason to go elsewhere; moreover, beyond Oxford's new walls a variety of different economic factors had been at work during the twelfth century. The Domesday population was increasing. In an underpopulated countryside, new villages were being established and monasteries founded as well as urban growth deliberately stimulated. Against this background of urban expansion throughout the area, Oxford's powerful weavers' guild was decreasing in importance. Some of the earliest fulling mills to be introduced into England were established in the county, at Seacourt by 1200, at Brightwell and Clevely in 1208 and two at Witney by 1223. The machine needed water power, so industry followed it into the countryside. The richest areas of the region became those in reach of water power. Even small villages became 'industrial' centres, as the villages along the Sor Brook in the north long remained. At the same time these movements stimulated trade and the agricultural wealth of the western fringes in particular was reinforced. The new routes for goods which could no longer come by river but had to be carried overland gave importance to a different set of distributing centres. To the documented pre-Conquest markets at Bampton, Abingdon and Wallingford, and to the newly developed twelfth century market towns, were added many others; Adderbury and Faringdon in 1218, Chipping Norton in 1224, Standlake and Stanford in the Vale in 1230, Bicester in 1239. Between 1245 and 1272 another seven towns received the formal grant of a market – Islip, Whitchurch, Watlington, Great Rollright, Charlbury, Henley, Radcot – and lastly Wantage in 1285. By the fourteenth century the impetus was exhausted; there were only three grants, to Stratton Audley in 1318, to Churchill in 1327 and to Bignell in 1377. The two lastcomers were East Hendred in 1415 and Hook Norton in 1435. Some of these places also had the right to hold a fair, an annual event to which people came from much further afield, bringing for sale a far wider selection of goods.

Although the formal grant of market rights may in several cases have been only the regularisation of an existing situation, nevertheless the privilege, once obtained, was jealously guarded. In the 1180s the men of Oxford and Wallingford had protested vigorously about competition from Abingdon Abbey's market in Abingdon. The abbot was forbidden to sell goods brought by water unless they had been carried in his own boats. Later, the abbots had an even more long drawn out argument with the earl of Wantage over rights to a fair at Shellingford. In 1212 the abbot was summoned before the king's courts to show what right he had to a fair at Shellingford, the earl having complained that it was prejudicial to his fair at Wantage. The abbot claimed that neither he nor his men had taken toll. He was temporarily restrained from holding his fair. In 1221, however, he succeeded in obtaining a charter giving him rights for a limited period on condition that he paid the amercements or fines to the king. Fifty years later the dispute broke out afresh when the lord of Wantage manor was accused of slaying a man at Shellingford fair and forcing all those frequenting it to go to his own fair at Wantage. In the end both parties were satisfied by a reissue of grants confirming separate rights, the one to have a fair at Faringdon, the other at Wantage. Shellingford's fair disappeared.

Even without such complicated troubles there were several markets which failed, either because they lay too close to each other, or because they were competing against a much larger centre nearby. Thus Deddington competed with Banbury, Radcot with Bampton and Faringdon, Standlake with Eynsham, Stratton Audley and Middleton Stoney with Bicester. Those markets which did succeed were mostly those in older urban centres, and these towns, roughly twelve miles apart, became, as they have remained, focal points in quite heavily settled countryside, where increase of population resulted in the creation of new settlements. Some of the earliest lay in or on the edges of Wychwood Forest; Finstock (1135), Ramsden (1146), Fawler (1205), Crawley (1214), and Hailey 1240. Here, three separate settlements are now represented in Middle Town, Delly End and Poffley End. Deep within the forest lay Leafield, first mentioned in 1213. On the wooded Chiltern slopes Nuffield had become a separate parish by 1183, severed from the royal manor of Benson, and Woodcote in 1109.

In the eastern part of the county Caulcott was an offshoot from Lower Heyford, in existence by 1199 and supporting a larger population than its parent village until the end of the fourteenth century. Its houses lie along an unusually narrow street, in strong contrast to the sprawl of its parent village, reflecting its deliberate creation. Fewcott, Murcott, Fencott, and perhaps also Willaston, were new foundations set in newly cleared land. Little

Chesterton grew from the mid-twelfth century as a result of more intensive land exploitation by ecclesiastical landowners. Newton Purcell existed by 1198 and later generated its own hamlet of Newton Morrell.

At much the same time the Thames flood plain was being drained and the villages of Northmoor, Standlake and Hardwick (Cokethorpe) grew up. Further west Upton near Burford is first recorded in 1200 and Signet in 1285. Brookend, lying beyond the present village of Chastleton, first appears between 1152 and 1200, brought into existence by the expanding need for food at Eynsham abbey; by 1279 the village consisted of sixteen households.

The people who founded towns and obtained grants of markets or fairs were the same kind of people who, in the twelfth century, founded monasteries. Only one foundation survived from before the Conquest, that at Abingdon, the only monastery in the Vale. Two which had been deserted were refounded; Benedictine Eynsham (1094) and St Frideswide at Oxford (1122). Members of the new Norman nobility established others; Robert D'Oilli II at Oseney in 1129, Gilbert Bassett at Bicester around 1140, Nicholas Bassett at Bruern in 1137, Bernard of St Valery at Studley around 1176 and Magister Michael Belet, son of Henry II's butler, at Wroxton in 1218. The last foundation was that of Edmund, earl of Cornwall, cousin of king Edward I, at Rewley on the outskirts of Oxford around 1281.

There were at least ten others, whose founders are now forgotten; the Benedictine priory at Wallingford and nunneries at Godstow, Studley and Littlemore, the Augustinian foundations at Dorchester, Cold Norton, and a nunnery at Goring and Cistercian Offley in Oddington. The Knights Templar had a house at Sandford on Thames and the Knights Hospitaller at Clanfield. Three priories belonged to monks whose mother house was in France; Cogges, Minster Lovell and Steventon.

The site of Abingdon, its gatehouse still watching over the market place, is the only guide to the size of the largest foundations. Virtually nothing survives of the smaller houses. The Trout Inn at Wolvercote and the Shaven Crown in Shipton under Wychwood are both said to have been guesthouses, one of Godstow, the other of Bruern, whose east window is now in Chipping Norton's church. Better fortune attended outlying monastic buildings which had a value to later farmers outweighing the odium associated with monastic centres. Several granges of Abingdon Abbey are easily recognisable; one is now a church on Northcourt Road, Abingdon, another forms part of Culham Manor, a third stands next the church at Charney Bassett, a fourth is incorporated in Dean Farm, Cumnor.

Abingdon Abbey was exceptional. Longest established, it had had most opportunity to attract donations. Foundations near Oxford also attracted gifts more readily than the rural monasteries, many of which remained small. Founders did not always give their best land. Piety was not allowed to prejudice their own profit. Bruern took its name from the heathland on which it was built; the house at Oddington was so poorly sited on marshy ground that it was moved to Thame ten years after its establishment. The poor land with which many others too were endowed was fit at the time of its donation only for sheep grazing. It was sheer chance that this later became advantageous and that much later monastic wealth was based on wool.

Nevertheless the amount of land in the county given to the religious houses was very large. The surviving records of five local houses – Abingdon, Eynsham, Godstow, St Frideswide's and the Hospital of St John – show how few villages were untouched by at least one ecclesiastical landlord. Other foundations, whose mother house was beyond the county boundaries, might also hold land in the area. One such was Beaulieu Abbey in Hampshire which was given Faringdon and Great Coxwell by king John early in the thirteenth century. They established a large farm at nearby Wyke while their barn at Great Coxwell shows how much the monks expected their lands to yield; 152 feet long and 44 feet wide (46 x 13.41 m), the roof of Cotswold stone tiles is carried still on the original oak posts at a height of 48 feet (14.63 m). The posts rest on stone bases nearly 7 feet (2.1m) high, capped with oak plates laid sideways to prevent damp from the stone rising into the posts. The monk in charge lived in a loft above the west porch, since destroyed. Reading Abbey was another great owner in the Vale; its barn at Manor Farm Cholsey, 355 feet (108 m) long, was the largest in Europe. Its modern successor, not quite as enormous, is nevertheless impressive.

The monasteries were inevitably absentee landlords, their representative, as far as the village was concerned, a bailiff, from whose accounts it is occasionally possible to reconstruct both management principles and day to day details of farming practice. This, however, establishes a key point in the area's history. The absentee institutional landlord who held a high percentage of exploitable land in the area was the agent in the creation of wealth, Abingdon Abbey in the Vale, Eynsham Abbey in Oxfordshire. The management of Oseney abbey's sheep flocks suggest centralisation with increased efficiency the objective.

The monks were not the only absentee landowners. Oxfordshire was covered by large areas of royal forest which only slowly shrank from their Domesday sizes. The medieval bounds of the two largest are known. Both had royal hunting lodges sited around their fringes, Beckley and Islip attached to Shotover and Stowood forest, Woodstock, Langley, Finmere and Cornbury round Wychwood. Every medieval monarch made use of them. Edward the Confessor was born at Islip, Richard of Cornwall and Edward the Black Prince at Woodstock, where Henry II had also spent a lot of time. His son Richard the Lionheart was born in Oxford. The royal presence, and the presence·of the court, may account for the superior quality of life in the county throughout the middle ages. Oxfordshire was consistently the territory of the well-to-do and influential even if, although the title earl of Oxford existed, the earl's lands were not in the county.

Royal influence made itself felt even more through the king's representatives. The ever increasing burden of administration fell on the lesser men, people like the Barentynes of Chalgrove, the de Malyns of Chinnor and the prolific Fettiplaces. One such man, Sir Edmund Chelrey of Childrey, quietly built up an estate of six manors, serving on innumerable commissions of investigation and acting as a justice of the peace. He died rewarded with a knighthood, having also established a chantry chapel in his parish church. The tombs of such men are to be seen in the churches. Sir Edmund's neighbour at Sparsholt stands in full-size wooden effigy between his two wives; Sir Robert Fitzwarin, Knight of the Garter, and his grandson lie in Wantage, Crusading Holcott reclines in Dorchester while at Long Wittenham the tiny figure of a knight who did not return from Crusade lies under a trefoiled canopy erected by his sorrowing widow. At Great Tew an odd couple, he a knight, she an abbess of Godstow, lie in their separate tombs.

These men and women's wealth and interests are very visibly demonstrated in the many village churches, built, reconstructed, added to and embellished continuously according to changing fashions. Church building had been another of the ways in which the Normans had stamped their presence on the countryside, probably the biggest change to the landscape they made, being more widespread than the castles they scattered across it. Thirty-one churches were recorded in the Domesday survey of the Vale and may be presumed to be Saxon foundations. The commissioners had no obligation to record a church and did not do so in Oxfordshire. It has been estimated that here the Normans inherited some one hundred and eighty churches many of which, given the paucity of surviving Saxon work, were probably of timber. A century after the Conquest another eighty churches had been built. Few complete examples survive. The gem stands at Iffley, its west door carved with jagged dogtooth surmounted by signs of the zodiac and the emblems of the Evangelists below a circular window. There are others at Upton near Blewbury, Letcombe Bassett and Cassington.

The pre-Reformation church liturgy separated priest from people, allowed, possibly even encouraged, the veneration of saints at side altars and did not, until relatively late in the fourteenth century, place much emphasis on preaching. The buildings that evolved to accommodate these liturgical needs thus required an area separately entered and reserved for the exclusive use of the priest, the chancel. Here the sacred vessels could be stored in a cupboard (aumbrey), and rinsed, over the piscina, and seats, sedilia, were provided for the celebrants and assistants. In addition to the altar there might be an Easter Sepulchre in which the Holy Oils and the Sacrament were placed between Good Friday and Easter Day and any reliquary which the church was fortunate enough to possess, as for example, at Stanford. All this, however, was shut off from the congregation by a screen, the rood screen. Worshippers stood rather than sat through a service about whose progress they were informed by the tinkling of the Sanctus bell, their own prayers offered to the saints whose altars were on the side walls.

Church plans vary; some of the earliest had an apsidal (semicircular) east end, but most, whatever their layout now, started with a linear building divided into rectangles of chancel and nave. Western towers were late additions; where there is a central tower it is often the survival from an older building. It is rare to find a whole church dated to a single period. The thirteenth century is represented at Uffington, the fourteenth at Broughton and West Hendred, the fifteenth at Combe, Rycote, Ewelme and Minster Lovell. Certain elements, however, appear consistently and the study of one, North Leigh, illustrates the features of all.

The Saxon church had a central tower, which survives now as the tower at the west end. The Saxon chancel lay on its east side while the nave extended to the west; the roofline of a steeply pitched, high and narrow nave can be seen on the outer western face of the tower. Both nave and chancel were pulled down by the Normans who replaced only the nave, unusual in that it was aisled and thus became wider than the tower. Its new entrance is the present south doorway. Around 1280 the present chancel was added, longer and narrower than the nave, also with a steeply pitched roof whose timbers can still be seen. The fashion for chantry chapels, served by a priest paid to say masses for the souls of the builder and his family, was around one hundred and fifty years old by 1442 when the Wilcote chantry was built by extending the north aisle to almost the same length as the chancel.

In common with most other churches no work was carried out in the sixteenth century. In 1690 the final addition to the building was made, the Perrot Aisle, built parallel to the north aisle. Meantime the church had been decorated with wall paintings, and had acquired brasses, tombs and stained glass. As in almost every other church, the nineteenth century restorers were here, in this case with a light hand.

These then were the usual elements of any church; the separate parts may vary widely in size and quality. One reason for this lies in the sharing of responsibility for maintenance between the landowner (the chancel) and the parish (the nave) on which the churchwardens could levy a rate. Some landowners were generous – Reading Abbey at Cholsey, the dean of Salisbury at Blewbury, Abingdon Abbey at Uffington and, later, New College at Adderbury. Others were clearly not, for example at Horley where the Norman chancel and tower are markedly different from the vast aisled nave built in the fourteenth century. During the thirteenth century the clergy were trying to make clear the difference between themselves and the laity, a difference which could be emphasised by rebuilding the chancel to make it more magnificent than the nave. Stanton Harcourt, rebuilt about 1250, where even the original screen survives, is one such case. Great Chesterton, Sandford St Martin, Bucknell and Langford are others. The size of the nave, however, might be increased by wealthy laymen, usually the lord of the manor, adding on a chantry chapel in which he would then be buried and in which masses for his soul would be said. Examples are at North Moreton, Mapledurham, Somerton and East Hagbourne where its builders, man and wife, lie buried.

Throughout its medieval existence the church was a place of colour, seen not just in wall paintings and glass, but also in painted woodwork of the screen, the painted images of saints in plaster or wood and in priests' garments. We are left with only the barest idea, and it is in looking for detail that one finds the best. Carving was the most common form of decoration, most obvious in the rounded doorways of Norman date, some of which were further embellished with carved lintels, for example at Church Hanborough, Fritwell, Great Rollright, Charney Bassett, Barford St Michael and Kencot. Pagan and Christian images mingle; Sagittarius the archer guards the entrance to Kencot and appears also on the font at Hook Norton with other signs of the zodiac alongside the Christian symbolism of Adam and Eve. Other fonts of the same period were more conventional, at least in appearance; the rare lead fonts at Childrey, Long Wittenham and Dorchester were decorated with figures of bishops or apostles in relief. On exteriors carving might be less reverent, displaying rather more joy in living, like the animal friezes and capital heads of Adderbury, Alkerton, Bloxham and Hanwell. Wood, whether in screens, misericords, beams or rafters, was also carved.

Much of what decorated the medieval church was given and paid for by the local lord, its workmanship a testimony not only to his wealth and taste but to the skills on which he could call; stonemason, painter, plasterer, carpenter, glazier, glassmaker, embroiderer and brass founder were all pressed into service. Most of the craftsmen remain anonymous; we do not even know if they were local men. They are commemorated only by the skill of their hands; with others whose only appearance is in court records, caught for their misdemeanours, they lie in unmarked graves. Nevertheless, it was for them that the narrative stories depicted in stained glass or painted on walls were devised, though of course such paintings might also commemorate their donor or, more rarely, contemporary events. Paintings at Chalgrove, Black Bourton and Shorthampton stuck strictly to biblical stories; those at South Newington depict both the suffering of Jesus, the execution of the much loved Thomas of Lancaster and has figures of the donors, rather larger than any of the others. At North Moreton the donors kneel either side of the resurrected Christ.

Carving, or later, engraving on brass, was especially fine on tombs, whether for priests like Sire John Hotham graduate of the Queen's College, Oxford at Chinnor, the unidentified knight at Childrey, king Henry V's winetaster at Whitchurch, or the merchants of Witney and Chipping Norton. Those who built the great houses made sure also that there was a memorial in the church; thus Sir John de Broughton lies in the church outside his castle, Sir Robert Bardolph in his chantry at Mapledurham, Sir John de Grey at Rotherfield Greys and his daughter at Stanton Harcourt.

Though much of the medieval decoration was smashed at the Reformation or later, often more survives in the church than of the dwellings of its donors. Like the church, the earliest houses were rebuilt or extended, each addition concealing or requiring the destruction of what preceded it. Three fourteenth century houses survive, Broughton, Stonor and Greys Court, not always in their original form, to demonstrate the development from the simple halls at Appleton and Sutton Courtenay.

The core of Broughton, dated to the mid-thirteenth century, was a square fortified manor house on the site of the present chapel and parlour. About fifty years later the present Great Hall was added, linked to the earlier structure by a vaulted corridor, the work carried out for Sir John de Broughton who, as a knight of Edward I, had served both abroad and against the Scots. He also built a tower, south of the chapel. On the other side of the hall lay the kitchen. All were surrounded by a moat, providing a defensive character.

At much the same time one of the other major families, the Stonors, who increased the size of their estate eight times over between 1086 and 1279 by piecemeal purchase of small parcels of land, were building their earliest surviving house at Stonor Park. It dates to between 1280 and 1300, and was a stone two-aisled hall with its northern end running into the hillside and its southern end flanked by a two-storeyed wing containing service rooms on the ground floor and a private room, the solar, above. The detached chapel was probably added about twenty years later.

Such houses were the residences of those with large numbers of dependents to feed, not just an extended family, but armed retainers and the servants needed to run both the household and the estates. Estates for which such buildings were the administrative centre might also possess other means to supplement food supplies, for sowing crops was not the only source of food. For both lord and monk it might also be provided from deer parks, fishponds, rabbit warrens and dovecotes. Survivals of the last are rare; Minster Lovell boasts a circular example. Leland mentions Abingdon Abbey's 'very fine rabbit warren' and another at Stonor. Fishponds, very differently distributed from Domesday fisheries, are more frequent; some fifty-one examples have been listed, the best being at Broughton Castle, Stanton Harcourt, Barford St Michael and Hanwell. They were deliberately stocked, usually with pike, bream, roach and perch.

Although the main purpose of the deer park was to give the lord a private hunting ground without infringing forest law which reserved game for the king, it was also a source of fresh meat. They were stocked with red, fallow and roe deer, in that order of preference. In 1201 Gerard de Camville received a gift of royal buck and does to stock the park he had been permitted to create near his castle at Middleton Stoney. Its 1328 boundary now survives as a bank and ditch round Home Wood within the much enlarged park laid out in 1825. Kirtlington's 'new park' of about seventy-five acres (30 ha) is recorded in 1279 while in 1322 Roger Damory at neighbouring Bletchingdon also had a park. Many more existed in the Chilterns, amongst them Ewelme, Mapledurham, Rotherfield Greys and Stonor.

In the Vale the earliest seems to have been that of the abbot of Abingdon at Radley; others were created in East Hendred, Kingston Lisle, Compton Beauchamp and at Wicklesham southeast of Faringdon. Another, belonging to the abbot of Glastonbury, lay within Ashdown parish; its boundary ditch and embankment, which would have been surmounted by a six foot (2 m) fence, is still to be traced round Upper Wood.

These adjuncts made a residence more than usually self-supporting. Some owners made efforts at fortification. The fourteenth century saw the construction of four fortified dwellings, all to the same fashionable design, a square enclosure protected by circular towers at each corner. This was the original plan of Greys Court, not immediately recognisable now, for which Sir John Grey received permission to fortify in 1344; a similar building had been erected by Aymer de Valence, earl of Pembroke, at Bampton in 1315. At much the same time the bishop of Lincoln remodelled his castle at Banbury on similar lines. Licence to fortify was granted to Warin de Lisle for a castle at Shirburn in 1377; his rectangular brick structure is now incorporated in the present house.

Although none of the defensive precautions was really necessary, the county was a restless place in the fourteenth century. In 1311/12 Piers Gaveston, the foreign favourite of king Edward II, was briefly imprisoned at Deddington, before being captured by his enemies and executed. Abingdon men captured royal officials at Oseney Abbey near Oxford; captured in their turn, the rebels admitted that collections had been organised to pay for the dirty work to be done. In 1327 they went further still, shutting the abbot of Abingdon into his own, then unprotected, abbey, burning the bell tower and smashing up the town. Minor lawlessness was common, but the area was too far inland to suffer from the frequent, and more damaging, raids made by the French along the south coast. The fortified residences were less a necessity than a demonstration of the wealth which existed by the early fourteenth century.

In 1334 a new basis of taxation was set out. Oxfordshire, yielding roughly 38s. 10d. per thousand acres (405 ha), appeared as the richest county in England; Berkshire, yielding 29s. 5d., the third. The distribution of that wealth is not substantially different from that of Domesday Book; the poorest area was still the Chiltern zone, followed by central Oxfordshire; the Vale, the Oxford Heights and Banbury were the next wealthiest, but the most prosperous area centred on Bampton and Burford, where taxable wealth was almost four times as much as in the Chilterns. Eight or nine generations of expansion had witnessed both an increase in the number of settlements and in the number of inhabitants, even though many villages remained small in size. Only five had over one hundred and fifty inhabitants, 35% had between ten and thirty-nine, the majority five to nine.

Recovery to Reformation 1348-1536

The prosperity revealed by the tax assessment of 1334 presents a picture one might expect to change with the advent of the great plague, the Black Death, which reached England in 1348. In some places its effects were clearly devastating; at Newton Purcell, for example, six rectors were recorded between 1348 and 1354. Only two villages were completely wiped out; Tilgarsley in Eynsham, where, within ten years, even memory of the site had faded, and Tusmore, where in 1354 the lord was given permission to empark the village site because all his villeins had died. Overall the plague probably killed around a third of the total population, sufficient to cause some, though remarkably little, dislocation, more than sufficient to jolt landlords into devising new means of exploiting their lands. Although numbers of deserted villages certainly increased from 1348 onwards, it is clear that most survived the immediate effects of the plague, only to fall victim to different methods of farming. A decrease in numbers of labourers could be overcome by turning arable land, which required considerable manpower to cultivate, into grazing because supervision of sheep required only one man for several large flocks.

In the hundred years following the first of many outbreaks of plague, some twenty-five villages in Oxfordshire were deserted, between 1450 and 1700 forty more. The wooded areas of the Chilterns, infertile Otmoor and the very rich lands of the north suffered least; woodland could be used for grazing, while a marriage of ploughland and pasture might not be more profitable used only for grazing. It was on marginal or exhausted land that villagers suffered most. Lack of documentation precludes our knowing much about the medieval enclosing landlord, but the ecclesiastical owners in Oxfordshire were responsible for roughly 25% of the total number of desertions. In some instances, where the unit was neither practicable nor profitable, there might be good reason and little hardship in removing a village. At Brookend in Chastleton, created during the twelfth century, decline was gradual. Houses left empty by the plague were inhabited by others; the monastic overlord was happy to let men move away, provided they paid their dues first; indeed those wishing to leave were assisted to enter the church. But by 1441 Brookend had dwindled to only three families 'the rest having gone away by night with their goods and chattels to a neighbouring village'. Consolidation of land into the hands of a few, together with diminishing yields from over exploited soil, gave the monks every inducement to turn low-yielding arable into profitable pasture.

At Asterleigh, north of Woodstock, it was the decision of the landowner to build a house on a different site that removed the village from the map. It was deprived of parish status in 1466 because the emoluments were so diminished as to be insufficient to support a rector, or even a competent parochial chaplain, 'on account of paucity of parishioners, barrenness of land, defects of husbandry, and an unusual prevalence of pestilences and epidemic sicknesses'.

Detailed studies of three other villages – Thomley and Wretchwick both close to Bicester, and the Domesday prosperous village of Seacourt – show a similar pattern in which the Black Death was only the indirect cause of desertion. Seacourt was given 50% relief on its tax assessment of 1351, suggesting that it was hard hit; in 1428, the date of the next surviving tax list, it was not even mentioned. In 1439 the vicar petitioned that the church be pronounced without a parish. Thomley's population of about one hundred and fifty had dwindled by 1377 to a mere thirty people over fourteen, the empty cottages first mentioned in 1349 still unfilled, the land still untilled.

In the fifteenth century Bicester Priory, faced with a shrinking population on its land at Wretchwick, consolidated its holdings in the open fields and hedged them in so that sheep and dairy cattle could graze under minimum supervision. In 1489 another prior was accused of pulling down five houses, enclosing further arable land and putting three plough teams out of work. Altogether eighteen people lost their livelihoods.

The paradox is that the second half of the fourteenth and the entire fifteenth century show every indication of continuing, indeed of increasing and downward spreading wealth. At Woolstone, although there were some dips and troughs in the rentals of land there belonging to St Swithun's Winchester, the recipients did not really suffer a serious drop in income from having to pay wages for people to perform tasks that had once been done unpaid, as part of customary labour. The change from labour services to waged work seems indeed to have taken place in the region without undue upset. When, in 1381, East Anglia and the southeast of England were convulsed by the Peasants' Revolt, provoked by rural poverty because wages had been fixed at pre-plague rates while prices were rising rapidly, Oxfordshire seems to have raised only a token protest, although the constable of Wallingford Castle, Richard, acted as one of the lieutenants to the revolt's leader. In the harsh and heavy-handed aftermath, the king's justices sent to track down and sentence offenders were specifically instructed to

lay hands on seven named individuals from Abingdon. More serious vio-
lence occurred in 1396 when men of Bampton, Witney and Eynsham banded together, chose a captain and paraded through the countryside on Palm
Sunday chanting 'Arise, arise, all men and go with us, those who will not
shall all be dead'.

These were longer term effects of the plague. More immediate reactions
suggest that the life style of the seriously wealthy was little affected. About
1349, just after the first visitation, Sir John Stonor established a foundation
of chantry priests at Stonor. He enlarged the chapel, giving the priests
accommodation in the old hall and solar and possibly building extra rooms
so that chapel and living quarters were connected. For himself and his family he built, further west, a timber-framed hall with a two-storey wing at
each end. One contained a parlour on the ground floor and a solar above,
while the other sheltered the service rooms. Beyond them lay the kitchen.
In 1362 the house was described as a messuage with divers buildings and
dovecotes. It must have been fairly large, for in 1378 his grandson entertained three royal justices and their retinues. Though there was no further
building, the interior was 'done over' periodically. An inventory of 1464
mentions the hall with its hangings of black silk and the Little Chamber
adjoining the Parlour 'hanged with paled cloth of purple and green'.

Stonor's house was much the same size as the residence of the Bardolphs
at nearby Mapledurham, now used as a tea room. The Black Death does not
seem to have greatly affected their life style either, for we know of their
wealth, and the regard in which the rich held themselves, from the actions
of Sir Robert and Dame Amice Bardolph. The wills of both survive, Sir Robert's brief and businesslike arrangements for charitable bequests and the
disposition of the estate compensated for by the life-size brass of himself in
full armour still to be seen in the church. Dame Amice took more care over
the disposal of her personal possessions, giving us an insight into the manner in which she had lived. In 1416 her bequests included money to the
church of St Peter Westminster where she was buried, and to the church at
Mapledurham, as well as detailed, more personal gifts.

My red gilt vestment, with two frontals of the same cloth, two altar cloths, a
painted picture, a super-altar, a chalice, two cruets of silver and gilt with feet in
the base, to remain and serve in divine offices at the altar of the new chapel.

To Elizabeth my sister, 10 marks. To William Lynde my best coverlet with one
tester, one canopy, three curtains of the same colour, one pair of best sheets, two
blankets, one mattress, one canvas, one basin with ewer, one quart pot, one silver
'potelpot', two silver flat dishes, six dishes, six silver salts, two pieces with silver

covers, one silver piece without cover, and in money 10 pounds.

To James Lynde two flat dishes, six silver dishes, two pieces with two silver covers, one silver piece without cover, one basin with silver ewer, one second best coverlet with one tester, one canopy, three curtains of the same colour, one pair of sheets, second best, two blankets, two mattresses, one canvas and in money ten pounds.

To Joan Merston, my servant, two red coverlets embroidered with white feet in the centre with two testers, two canopies, two curtains of the same colour, being in London, one pair of sheets, two blankets, one mattress, one canvas, one white coverlet with blue stars, one cloak, one mantle furred with grey, one small chest bound with iron, two large brass pots now in London, one 'possenet', one pan, and all veils for my head of silk and linen, six dishes, six silver salts, which were wont to travel with me riding through the country, and in money 10 marks.

To John Upsale a bed, to wit, one coverlet with tester, one canopy, three curtains, two sheets, two blankets, two mattresses, one canvas, all of the best I possess after the beds above bequeathed by me; also my second best horse with saddle, bridle, and all its apparel, and in money 40s.

William and James Lynde were also to have all her vessels of lead, brass, and iron not bequeathed and all the chests at Mapledurham and in her hostel in London, equally divided between them. Other, smaller, bequests were arranged for servants and for the poor. A separate sum was set aside for the repair of the roads 'where most need is'.

For some of the Bardolphs' contemporaries, however, the decrease in the value of land after the Black Death, because there were fewer to work it and of necessity it lay fallow or because, in the towns, houses stood empty, was a situation which might be turned to advantage. William of Wykeham, born, according to his enemies, the son of a butcher, rose to become bishop of Winchester and chancellor of England. He bought up empty plots in the northeast corner of Oxford on which he founded New College. In the county he bought the manors of Broughton, Adderbury, Bloxham, Swalcliffe and Upper Heyford, transferring ownership to his college to provide an income In four places he built a huge stone barn to store the harvests. That at Upper Heyford is still in use at Church Farm, those at Adderbury and Bloxham have been converted to domestic use. The magnificent building at Swalcliffe, 134 feet long and 29 feet wide (40.84 x 8.83 m), is now a farm museum, open to the public. Some of the building accounts survive. Its construction, at a cost of around £180,000 in today's money, was organised by men who combined the interests of the locality with those of the college. Their faith in the continued productivity of the land was not long justified.

At Broughton Castle towards the end of the century and the end of his life William of Wykeham engaged in yet more construction. The space between the kitchen tower and the chapel was filled in by a high, vaulted loggia with a belvedere on top. He may also have been responsible for reconstructing the gatehouse which, though it has no portcullis, has two pairs of wooden doors and cross arrow slits. In 1406 a licence to fortify was given to his nephew, Sir Thomas Wykeham, who inherited. Sir Thomas may have built both the battlemented wall which still stands between the gatehouse and the stables which, together with the still filled moats, give an impression of strength.

Fifty years later his grandson enlarged the castle still further. The hall was extended and the old kitchen replaced by a full range of service rooms whose external walls stand today as the shell of the west wing. At the same time the private rooms in the east wing were remodelled to make them more easily defensible. They are represented now by the twisting stone stair leading to the bedroom which has a squint to allow its occupants to look into the chapel.

Economies of manpower, expansion of grazing flocks of sheep to replace ploughland, and good marriages were the basis of wealth, at least in the countryside. In 1475 William Stonor increased his fortune by marrying Elizabeth Ryche, daughter of a London merchant with connections in the wool trade, conferring higher social status on his bride. It was not an entirely successful union; his family regarded her as a parvenue, while she, theoretically in charge of the estate during her husband's many business trips, does not seem to have been possessed of any of the practical skills that might have been expected of a merchant's daughter. Their correspondence reveals a naively extravagant girl, much in need of the guidance of her husband's steward.

Elizabeth had moved from a cramped London house to more spacious, but old fashioned, Stonor. More typical large fifteenth century houses are at Minster Lovell and Stanton Harcourt, both examples of the newer style courtyard house. The absence of defences indicates peace and continuing prosperity in the countryside; the courtyard house also demonstrates the increasing differentiation between the lord and his family from servants and retainers, accommodated elsewhere and no longer sharing the hall. This was the sort of house built at Minster Lovell by William, seventh baron Lovell, on his return from fighting the French in the Hundred Years War in 1431. He decided to demolish the twelfth century house and church and to build anew, making use of stone from both, as well as from the small priory of foreign monks which, like that at Cogges, had been dissolved some years earlier. Between the church and the river he built on three sides of a square, using the river to close the fourth. The main block consisted of the great hall, the chapel and the solar. Further accommodation, kitchens, bakehouse and stables occupied the two long wings; beyond was the circular dovecote and other outbuildings. Roofless now, the hall stood 45 feet long and 36 feet high (13.71 x 10.97 m); it was originally lit by large traceried windows filled with stained glass. It was probably heated by a central hearth, for there are no traces of fireplaces; ventilation may have been provided by openings in the gables. Entrance to the screens passage, separating kitchens from the hall, was through a fine porch on the north side, now ruinous. Behind the raised dais at the far end of the hall, on which the lord and his family sat for meals, were two small doors, one to the chapel, the other to the lord's private room, the solar, reached up a spiral stair. This too had a large glazed window and was heated by a fireplace, topped by a hexagonal chimney.

The present house at Stanton Harcourt is a nineteenth century rebuilding of sixteenth century stables and gatehouse, the upper window over the archway almost the only original feature. Not certainly dated and difficult to visualise because it was destroyed in the eighteenth century, the medieval house lay across the present gardens. The northern block of the quadrangle, containing the Great and Little Parlours, stood in line with the tower and the chapel, which marks the northeast corner. As at Broughton, the Harcourt family could enter the chapel from the upper floor of their own quarters, to sit in the gallery above their servants who entered from ground level. A block of rooms once adjoined the chapel on its southern side, while the present dovecote and the adjacent farm outbuildings mark the line of the south wing. The farmhouse next to the Great Kitchen was once service rooms in the west wing; beyond this range, and quite separate from the house to minimise the risk of fire, stood the Great Kitchen, best described in the words of a seventeenth century antiquary:

> it is so strangely unusual... for below it is nothing but a large square and octangular above ascending like a tower, the fires being made against the walls and the smoke climbing up them without any tunnels or disturbances to the cooks; which being stopped by a large conical roof at the top, goes out at loopholes on every side according as the wind sits; the loopholes on the side next the wind being shut with falling doors and the adverse side opened.

The ornamental ponds now enclosing two sides of the complex, self-supporting like all the others discussed, were once fishponds.

Both Stanton Harcourt and Minster Lovell reveal the fifteenth century's prosperity, which was little damaged by the Wars of the Roses, fought

Left: Minster Lovell Hall

Below: Wickens Store, East Hendred

Below: The Mill, Mapledurham

Below right: Kelmscott Manor

Above: Wroxton Abbey

Right: The dovecote, Chastleton

Below: Broughton Castle

between supporters of the rival claimants to England's throne, which broke out in 1459. The county was spared physical disturbance, but the Lovells, Harcourts, Stonors and Wykehams were all involved. Two Yorkists died in 1471; Wykeham of Broughton and Sir Robert Harcourt, High Steward of Oxford University. His grandson changed sides and acted as standard bearer to the Lancastrian Henry VII, fighting against his neighbour at Minster Lovell, Francis, grandson of the builder, whose estates were forfeited after the Lancastrian victory of 1485. Around 1482 Francis had solicited the help and support of William Stonor for the Yorkists, but Stonor, despite his third wife's Yorkist connections, opted to join a rebellion against king Richard. Stonor was pardoned by the victorious Lancastrian king, Henry VII, but nevertheless thought it prudent to display his loyalty by fighting against a Yorkist pretender at the battle of Stoke in 1487. Even then, the danger was not quite over; a second pretender, whose widow, Lady Katherine Gordon, lies buried at Fyfield, had yet to be defeated.

The last fortified building, Hanwell Castle, was erected after the end of the fighting for the Lancastrian victor's treasurer, Anthony Cope. Begun in 1498, the rounded corner turrets defending its rectangular core would have had little military value. Under attack, whether from a distance or from the high ground that overlooks it, they would have crumbled immediately. The design harked back to earlier times, the material, brick in a stone-quarrying region, a testimony to the prestige of the material and the man who paid for it.

By then it was not only the landed gentry who could afford grand buildings. Townsmen too were becoming both richer and better organised, far better able to look after their own interests than they had been at the time of the abortive disturbances at Abingdon in the 1320s. Though their shops and houses only rarely survive, like the Birdcage Inn at Thame and a shop where Ship Street joins Cornmarket in Oxford, their public buildings do. Abingdon townsmen in the Guild of St Helen built the bridge over the Thames in the town centre and the bridge at Culham over the Swift Ditch, both around 1415, to help the through trade of their town. About thirty years later they erected the Christchurch almshouses behind their church of St Helen in which they had already built a chantry chapel and installed the magnificent painted wooden ceiling. At Henley around 1400 the citizens had felt the need of a school and erected the three-storey timber building beside the church for this purpose. At the end of the century they too built almshouses for their poorer members, as the Deddington guild had also done.

Almshouses were more and more frequently built in this century. The finest example is the duchess of Suffolk's foundation at Ewelme, a church, almshouses and a school, begun in 1437. The church, begun about 1430 and finished within twenty years, has been little altered since her son commissioned and placed two tombs there. One was for his mother, the other for his grandparents, Thomas Chaucer, son of the poet Geoffrey, and his wife Matilda Burgersh through whom the Chaucers inherited Ewelme manor. Both these tombs are splendid examples of late fifteenth century work. Alice herself lies clad in the robes of the Order of the Garter, the only woman in the county to have held the honour.

To the church Alice added thirteen almshouses, of two rooms each, facing onto a square cloister, a well at its centre. The statutes provided for a corporation of two chaplains and thirteen poor men, having a common seal. One of the chaplains was to be the Master, paid ten pounds a year and living in rather larger quarters than his charges. His duties were defined, as were those of the 'poor men'. They were to wear cloaks with a red cross on the breast and to attend chapel twice a day. They received £3 6s.8d. a year. 'Poor men' was probably never taken absolutely literally; a nearer interpretation of the intentions of the foundress might be 'distressed gentlefolk'.

For the villagers the duchess built a large hall for use as a school; its Master, the second chaplain, was also provided with a house and a salary of £10 per year, for he was to teach 'freely without exaccion of any Schole hire'. The building is still in use, its original height now subdivided to make two floors, the Master's room still serving its original purpose.

On a lesser scale others too built chantries; Sir Richard Quatremayns erected the small church at Rycote in 1449 and Sir John Golafre built an almshouse, now the White Hart inn at Fyfield, to house twelve bedesmen and a master to pray for his soul. Merchants did not forget the church either. The wool merchants of Burford erected the porch there. Chipping Norton's leading businessman, John Ashfield, is credited with the rebuilding of the nave; his tomb, and those of many of his fellows, are still to be seen there. Other wealthy laymen built, or rebuilt, church towers, for example at Henley, Chipping Norton, Little Rollright and Mollington.

Whereas laymen might more and more indulge in good works, the traditional providers withdrew to concentrate increasingly on themselves. More and more life in the monasteries came to resemble the life of the noblemen, the monks bonding with the county society, their vocational identity dissolved by increasingly worldly habits. The abbot of Thame saw no reason against doing up his parlour between 1530 and 1539 in the latest Renaissance style, complete with a frieze bearing his name and, for good measure, his initials on the ceiling beams and in plaster swags of fruit decorating the walls. At the Dissolution, when the annual income of every monastery in the country was most carefully assessed, Abingdon, with a net income of £1535, was nearly two and a half times richer than Oseney, second on the list. None of the other fourteen houses had an annual income exceeding £421.

The wealth of England was enormous, the subject of amazement even to the Venetian ambassador posted in London. The steadily spreading prosperity of Oxfordshire is revealed in the will made in 1499 by the Bampton priest, Richard Holcott, whose brass survives in the church. His bequests were many and included two to his college, Oriel, Oxford. He also gave his church forty shillings 'to amend the silver foot for the Cross'. More still went to friends and servants.

To Elizabeth Gew my best silver salt with cover, my six best spoons and a silver bowl. To William Symond a silver bowl and six spoons with scrolls. The utensils of my kitchen to my servants, Stephen Ferrent and Henry Ferrent; and to the said Henry six selected dishes, six porringers and saucers, and six pewter dishes. To William Newman half a dozen of my best pewter vessels. To Stephen Ferrent my best chest and my two best patens. To Lucy David 40s. To Henry Ferrant, my servant, my second entire bed and four sheets. To Helianor Hooge a pestle and mortar of brass.

To Master John Grede, my executor, my best lined cloak; to Master Robert Coke my second cloak and to Richard Hakelewe my green cloak. To Lucy David a cloak and to Alice Ferrent another cloak. To Henry Ferrent my best cloak not bequeathed and another one. To Stephen and Henry Ferrent a diaper tablecloth, another of plain cloth and a towel. To Alice Shepperd a tablecloth of plain cloth and the like to Agnes Tykford, Joan Bifylde and Joan Crippys. To Robert Corser a tablecloth and a towel and to Maud Turfray the same. To Christian Dalby a tablecloth, a towel and a pair of sheets. To every girl of the parish of Bampton who shall be married within the year, 12d.

To John Taylour *Magistrum Sentenciarum, Destructorium Viciorum* and *Concordanciam*. I bequeath my Bible to the high altar of the Blessed Mary, Oxford. To Robert Bifyld a feather bed which is in my storehouse. To Alice Baston two candlesticks and a stove. To Stephen Ferrent two basins, an old pitcher, a tin bowl and my two best candlesticks. To my godson Robert 40s. to find him at school.

The inventory of household goods which were to remain for his successors in the parsonage included the lead and brass furnace in the brewhouse, a trough and kneading board and all the tables, trestles, forms and a chair pertaining to the hall together with the green hangings, all the bedsteads and his best brooch.

The same picture of solid comfort is demonstrated in the brick and timber building known now as Wickens Store at East Hendred, where a central hall is flanked by two cross wings. Its owner's furnishings and possessions were probably very similar to those of the Bampton priest, their comfortable life style shared by many in the middle levels of society.

From Reformation to Civil War 1536-1649

The suppression of the monasteries touched the county first in 1524 when Cardinal Wolsey gave the order for the closure of Littlemore and St Frideswide's. Disguised as the need for reform, the real reason may have been a wish to divert their revenues to his foundation of Cardinal College, for which Wolsey took the buildings of St Frideswide's. It was a gentle prelude to the dissolution of all monastic houses, large and small, throughout England which took place between 1536 and 1539.

The physical destruction was most obvious in Oxford itself. The Carmelite, Dominican, Franciscan and Augustinian friaries outside the medieval walls were all pulled down, their stonework robbed. Three of the sites were acquired by laymen and long remained empty; the fourth was acquired by the city and sold some sixty years later to become the site of Wadham College. The four monastic colleges, also sited outside the town walls, were also suppressed; two of their sites being more quickly redeveloped as colleges, St John's and Trinity. Of the five monasteries, Rewley and Littlemore disappeared completely, Godstow was altered into a secular residence, while Oseney, the second largest Augustinian abbey in England, was for seven years preserved for use as the cathedral church of the newly-created bishopric of Oxford, the first bishop being the former abbot. But in 1542 Henry VIII decided to make the church of his foundation of Christ Church, previously Wolsey's Cardinal College, into the cathedral. The site of Oseney was leased to a clothier, obliged to permit the plunder of the stone for use at Christ Church.

Nothing now remains of Oseney and the only faint clue to monastic grandeur is to be gained at Abingdon, where the gatehouse built after the disturbances of 1327 stands at the edge of the town's market place. Within the former precinct the Theatre represents the Chapter House and the part beyond, the area in which stood the abbey church, one of the largest in England. The only other major monastic building to survive is at Dorchester, where the abbey church was bought by the uncle of the last abbot and presented to the townsfolk for continued use as their parish church. In Bicester the monastic church was pulled down, though the cloister and outbuildings were turned into a house, as they were also at Thame and Wroxton.

It was not only the monastic buildings that were lost, but also their material contents. The dispersal of these possessions, whether land or movable goods (which included lead from roofs, stone from buildings, panelling from parlours as well as jewelled cups, crosses and books) benefited a wide variety of people. If they were not pilfered, the smaller or perishable goods, such as books, hay, fodder and beasts were sold locally. Even small quantities of building material might be sold; £9 worth of stone from Wallingford Priory was bought for the repair of the bridge.

The longer and the shorter term effects of the dissolution of the monasteries were very different. The longer term effects – the break-up and redistribution of the estates and the dispersal of goods – were, perhaps, not entirely disastrous. The immediate effects were both harsh and obvious. The despoliation of the buildings took place with remarkable speed, their destruction with varying degrees of thoroughness. The dispersal of the community caused considerable disruption to 'social services'. The disappearance of charitable services to the poor, of provision of education to the young, of retirement homes for the elderly, and of guesthouses and inn service for travellers all left gaps in the social fabric which the newly secularised society had to devise ways of filling.

We are fortunate in being able to glimpse parts of mid-sixteenth century Oxfordshire through the eyes of John Leland, whose appointment as king's antiquary took him on lengthy journeys in laborious search for England's antiquities between 1538 and 1542. His jottings, though neither systematic nor comprehensive, provide the first account of the area.

Leland, rector of Great Haseley, eight miles from Oxford, described, with obvious approval, some of the houses in the south of the county, amongst them the 'fine, large old manor house with two courtyards' at Harpsden and the manor house at Ewelme where

> a fine outer courtyard is surrounded by buildings of brick and timber. The inner part of the house stands inside a good moat and is richly built of brick and stone. There is a magnificent hall, which has crossbeams of iron not of timber. The parlour adjoining is extremely fine and full of light, as are all the residential rooms in the house.

Leland's neighbour, Mr Barentyne, at Little Haseley, owned 'a most attractive mansion, with remarkably fine walks, as well as orchards and ponds'.

His words confirm the continuing existence in the county of the enormous wealth we have already seen, based on commerce and sustained by agriculture. It was to increase for the next hundred years. More and more people came to own possessions of value, more and more people came to live in dwellings of greater size and increased comfort. Perhaps most important of all, more individuals came to own land. Some part of the steadily increasing wealth was due to inflation; farmers were able to sell their products at rising prices without correspondingly higher overheads. A far more significant factor, however, was the downward spread of land ownership, for it is clear that anyone with an investment in land, however small, saw his income rise. The fact that a larger number of people came to own land was one consequence of the dissolution of the monasteries.

The process was virtually complete as Leland rejoiced over some of the abbey's manuscripts he saw at Abingdon. By then the more valuable possessions had been carted off to the royal treasury for resale and, impossible to trace, passed mostly to individuals. Similar treatment was given to the estates and it is their dispersal, through a new government department, the Court of Augmentations, which made the biggest contribution to the redistribution of wealth. Three royal officials made major acquisitions of Oxfordshire lands, but, surprisingly, most of the lands were sold off in small parcels and bought on the initiative of the would-be purchaser for the then current sale price of twenty years' purchase – twenty times the annual rent. Even more surprisingly, though three-quarters of the estates acquired by the Crown had been sold off by 1558, apparently with no depreciation of land prices, few of the initial purchasers retained ownership. Most of the estates were resold with ten or fifteen years in ever smaller parcels.

The results of such activity in the land market in Oxfordshire are also surprising. There is no detailed survey of purchasers but a quick count suggests that the estates passed almost entirely to individuals rather than to institutions such as the Oxford colleges. Any investment in land turned out to be a good investment and, from the 1540s, when the survival of wills and inventories allows us to measure personal wealth, about 60% of the population died leaving estates worth less than £20. By the 1590s only 30% were worth less than £20, while 8% were worth more than £100. By 1640 still fewer (20%) were worth less than £20 while those worth more than £100 had increased to 30%, figures that were to remain more or less constant until the end of the century.

Greater wealth coincided with a period of architectural innovation. Leland described the typical medieval house which, within thirty to forty years, had largely been superseded by the two-storey dwelling. The courtyard plan, best exemplified now in Oxford colleges but once, like Minster Lovell and Stanton Harcourt, the universal style of all large private residences, went out of fashion as the need to house large bands of retainers died and men sought to display their wealth and education. At first little more than a conversion, one or more floors divided the height of the medieval hall, the upper storey being divided into small rooms each with its window. Fireplaces were inserted into larger rooms and stairs, replacing the simple ladder, were devised to communicate between different levels.

Many of these adaptations of an older building have survived in farm houses; many of the new buildings in the more modern style were relatively small, for example Marcham Priory, the core of Lyford Grange and Kelmscott Manor. Here the ground plan was entirely traditional; the hall was divided from the kitchen by a screens passage. The rooms were given large fireplaces. On the outside, however, the influence of the newer fashions is much more obvious, shown in the large glazed and mullioned windows, the height and the tall gables on all sides.

Much new building, however, was the prerogative either of the older families, some of whom we have already met, or of the merchants, royal officials and men without roots in the county; these 'new men' more and more frequently, were buying property in the country. Amongst the royal officials were three of the largest post-dissolution landowners; Lord Williams at Thame, Henry VIII's Treasurer, George Owen, his physician, and Thomas Pope, Treasurer of the new Court of Augmentations. Born in Deddington, Pope bought the lands and site of Wroxton Priory, with which he endowed Trinity College, Oxford. Later came Sir Lawrence Tanfield, Lord Chief Baron of the Exchequer under queen Elizabeth, the builder of Burford Priory out of the ruins of the hospital there. Amongst the merchants were Thomas Pope's friend Thomas White, founder of St John's College, Thomas Calton, a London goldsmith and purchaser of Milton Manor in 1548, John Latton purchaser of Kingston Bagpuize in 1566 and Thomas Coghill at Bletchingdon.

Local men followed the example of the 'new men' and some of the houses they built survive: of Thomas Horde at Cote (1553), of Walter Calcott, Staple Merchant and son of a burgess of Banbury at Williamscote (1560s), of another Staple Merchant, John Dormer at Steeple Barton (1570s), of Sir William Spencer at Yarnton, where the house was finished in 1612, and of Sir William Jones at Asthall (1620). Shipton Court, the house of the Laceys at Shipton under Wychwood, is on the H-plan with tall narrow gables and wide, well proportioned windows. Chastleton was built by the Witney wool merchant Walter Jones, purchasing the site from Robert Catesby who used the proceeds to finance the Gunpowder Plot to blow up the Houses of Parliament. Jones commissioned Robert Smythson, a leading architect, to design him a house which would display his wealth. The house is lofty, compact and square. A series of projecting towers and bays leads the eye up to the narrow gables which emphasise the building's height. Inside, the large rooms are lit by large windows, closed with glass, itself an expensive purchase. They were heated by fireplaces. The entrance hall is large and central, an echo of the medieval tradition, while on the topmost floor a long gallery, an Elizabethan innovation, runs the length of the building. Here, as elsewhere inside, money was spent lavishly on decoration: in plasterwork on the gallery's vaulted ceiling, in the great chamber on the first floor, which is fitted with carved panelling, or in the hall, where the screen is carved with acanthus scrolls, satyrs and half columns. The result was opulence and comfort.

Older families contented themselves with adding to the existing house. The most extravagant was Richard Fiennes at Broughton, where the house underwent two major rebuildings which transformed the moated castle into a magnificent home. The first phase of about 1540 raised the roof line of the medieval Great Hall in order to accommodate two extra floors, reached by stairs placed in two stair towers projecting from the rear of the building. State rooms filled the western wing, a great gallery on the second floor linking them to the smaller, private rooms in the east wing. Above the medieval kitchens Fiennes added two more rooms. The facade was improved by the insertion of large, symmetrical mullioned windows and two square bays. Inside, the architectural details of the public rooms are amongst the first to show the influence of the Italian Renaissance, best seen in the ceiling and fireplaces of the King's Chamber. Some thirty years later another three-storey wing was added to balance the earlier extensions; it housed the Great Parlour entered through the long gallery and gave the house its present appearance. It too was decorated with ornate plasterwork executed by the most skilled craftsmen that money could buy.

A second old-established family whom we have already met, the Stonors, also refurbished their already large house. Leland described for us the Stonor that he visited; in addition to its fine park and woodland and its rabbit warren he observed that 'the mansion has been built up against the hillside, with two courts of timber, brick and flint. The present owner, Sir Walter Stonor, has enlarged and strengthened the house, which has for a long time been in the possession of his family'. Yet within a generation extensive building was again under way. Between 1590 and 1600 the front, the east and west wings were rationalised, turned into a straight facade by filling in the hitherto irregular front. Elizabethan gables were added and large mullioned windows inserted. The old hall, whose blocked windows are still visible, was dismantled and its western half turned into a courtyard. The Long Gallery was built at the rear.

Stonor's neighbours, the Blounts of Mapledurham, went even further, moving out of their original manor house into the newly built H-plan house visited today. The new hall had rooms to either side, a stair turret at each end and, on the upper floor, gracious reception rooms, bedrooms and a long gallery. The medieval manor was left standing alongside and is now the tea room. Both the Stonors and the Blounts were Catholics; another family, the Fermors, built first at Somerton, then at Hardwick and finally in 1642 removed to Tusmore, where they built another, more splendid residence. At Lyford, the more modest Grange (not the house to be seen today) had only recently been built when in the 1580s it witnessed the capture of the Jesuit Edmund Campion.

The condition of the royal palace of Woodstock stood in strong contrast. Described in 1551 as 'decayed and prostrated', it was so dilapidated that 'in the hoole house there was butte three doores onelye that were able to be locked and barred'. Hasty repairs were carried out before the future queen Elizabeth could be kept prisoner in four refurbished rooms in the gatehouse, probably a structure like that still standing at Glympton, while her future subjects were beginning to live far more comfortably. Little wonder she later preferred to enjoy herself at Ditchley, albeit still in a house that was 'low, modest and with a bowling green'.

It was increasing wealth which made this building activity possible. In the 1540s most houses had three rooms or less. If by the end of the century half the population still lived the same way, 30% lived in four to six room dwellings and some 9% in seven or more rooms. By 1640 roughly 35% of the population lived in over seven rooms, around 30% in four to six rooms and 25% in less than three.

Much of this wealth was spread amongst the small landowners. It led to one of the major changes in the countryside, known now as the Great Rebuilding, because its scale was so massive. It concerned not only individual houses but sometimes, as in the case of Little Milton, the whole village, where prosperous yeomen farmers rebuilt their dwellings. There were, of course, other factors which forced reconstruction, amongst them fire. We know that at Oxford, Banbury and Bicester, much went up in flames. At Eynsham a fire on Whit Monday 1629 caused nearly £1000 worth of damage, destroying 101 'bays of building' (a bay is the unit of space between partition walls). Some of this probably represents barns, outhouses and stables, but the single largest loss totalled £200 and included four large houses, of twenty, seventeen, fifteen and twelve bays and a further eight houses ranging from one room cottages of one or two bays building to the commonest, six or seven bays, an average three room house. But much of the rebuilding of the later sixteenth and early seventeenth centuries came about through increased wealth, taking place first in the southern part of the area, while north of the Swere valley extensive rebuilding did not take place until after the Civil War.

Within a village there could be great differences in housing conditions. The contrast in wealth between the labourer and the yeoman farmer is vividly portrayed in two wills, one made by a farmer in Marston in 1593, the other made by a labourer of Taston in 1592. The farmer, Nicholas Hore, lived in a nine-roomed house and was undoubtedly amongst the wealthy, leaving a total of £386 10s. 8d. After his death his friends made an inventory of his goods, as they were required to do by law.

In the hall two tables, one cupboard, four joined stools, with glass and wainscot and other furniture in the same hall 40s.

In the parlour one joined bedstead, a featherbed and curtains, a flock bed, a round table with forms, 'seelings'(wainscot) and glass windows and also other implements £6

In the little chamber two chests with hemp and other implements 30s.

In the next chamber a bedstead, two coffers with wool, two coverlets, three blankets with other implements 30s.

In the chamber over the hall a joined bedstead, a featherbed, a coverlet, three blankets, a bolster, a pillow, a chest with other implements £3 13s. 4d.

In the chamber over the entry a bedstead, a featherbed, a coverlet, a quilt, two chests with other implements £4

In the maids' chamber one bed, a cupboard, two blankets, a coverlet with other implements 40s.

In the loft over the maids' chamber two beds, three coverlets, two blankets with other implements 40s.

A rack, eight sacks, two sheets with corn & other implements £3
In the kitchen and brewhouse tables, forms, cheese press with other implements 10s.

Brass pans, pots of brass and other implements £6

A furnace, settle, a mill and other implements £4

In the malthouse one vat with barley in the same 40s.

A cheese press, a stone and other implements 5s.

Forty quarters of malt appraised at £20

For lumber over the kitchen 10s.

Plough timber over the malthouse with other implements 26s.

In the little stable plough timber and cart timber 20s.

In the oxhouse one scaffold with beam timber 20s.

In the rickyard two hovels with beams and other things £3

Two loads of hay 20s.

Three ladders 6s.

One hovel with straw and other implements 40s.

Three carts with furniture thereunto, ploughs, gear, harrows, chains and yokes £5

One sheep house with racks and hovels £3

All the wood about the yard £12

Two ricks of wheat with hovel posts, standers and barley in the barn £45

Sheets, towels, tablecloths, napkins and other napery ware £13

Sheep racks and hurdles 7s.

Pewter dishes and other vessels 30s.

Four hundred sheep £150

Eight oxen seventeen kine £50

Five horse £10

Bacon 40s.

Fourteen hogs £4

Hens, geese and ducks 10s.

Seventeen acres of wheat on the ground £9

Barley and beans sown in the ground £10

Sum Total £386 10s. 8d.

On the other hand, Richard Churchhouse, labourer of Taston, could bequeath only 18s. 8d. worth of goods. His one-roomed hut contained a bed covering, three pairs of sheets and a bolster, a table cloth, two pots, two kettles, a frying-pan, two candlesticks, two platters, one porringer and a saucer, a cover (for the fire probably) a load of wood, a brandiron and other implements belonging to the house.

Richard was, however, lucky to hold onto his house; there were plenty who did not, for the new owners of land and the builders of the new houses further enriched themselves by continuing enclosure of the common land and, where necessary, the removal of villages. Thus the Fettiplaces at Eaton Hastings, the Wenmans at Carswell, and, most dramatically, the Poures at Bletchingdon, all went ahead to add to their fortunes, totally unrepentant about any hardship they caused. Challenged in a Star Chamber case, Sir William Barentyne, who had enclosed part of Clare, allegedly 'to the utter decay and desolation of the said town', replied threateningly to his accuser 'whoreson boy and false crafty knave, I will sit upon your skirts' and 'by many detestable oaths' promised to cut off his ears! The Poure family gradually enclosed about half of the three common fields at Bletchingdon between 1539 and 1596, the year when a crowd of villagers rioted. It was to no avail for the remaining thousand acres were finally enclosed, subdivided and hedged about in 1623 by the manor's new owner, Sir John Lenthall. Only the Cow Common, a few demesne acres and rough grazing on roadside verges, together with the green, remained open. The process is revealed now by the large farmhouses scattered on the outskirts of the parish, all of seventeenth century date. Elsewhere the old pattern might not be so dramatically changed, but the practice of enclosure too passed down the social scale as the second generation merchant climbed the social ladder.

All this added to the hardships of the poor. Tenant farmers at Standlake complained bitterly in 1625 when their village was overrun 'by a multitude of poor'. Not only, they said, were they losing poultry from their yards and the harvested corn from their fields, but they could scarcely keep 'any dead hedges a standing, but that they shall be taken away by night. And oftentimes their quick Mounds (hedges) and other trees, such as ashes, willows, etc., be pulled or cut up by the ground, to the great hurt of the owners who planted the same to their own use and public good'. The village, they said, was 'much overcharged with poor people placed in cottages and new erected tenements'. 'Hark, hark, the dogs do bark and the beggars are coming to town-oh' was a real enough cry.

Even when the beggars did come, they would not find much assistance. Leland's description of the bishop of Lincoln's town of Banbury was written just before the changes brought by the dissolution of the monasteries and the wave of new building; it is typical of the other small towns in the county where the lord's residence, the church and the market place were the dominant elements:

> Most of the town of Banbury lies in a valley, constricted on its northern and eastern sides by low-lying ground, partly meadow and partly marsh; on the south and southwest the land is rather higher than the site of the town itself. Banbury's best street is that which runs east-west down to the river Cherwell. At the western end of this street is a large open area surrounded with rather good buildings, and with a fine cross raised on several steps. A very celebrated market is held in this area every Thursday, and it is watered by a stream of fresh water.

> Another good street runs from south to north and at each end of it is a stone gate. There are other gates in the town, but there is no certainty that Banbury was ever ditched or walled. On the northern side of the town is a castle having two wards, each with a ditch. There is a fearsome prison for convicts in the outer ward, and in the northern part is a fine piece of new stone building...

> There is only one parish church, dedicated to Our Lady. It is a large building, most particularly it is broad. I saw only one notable tomb there, and that was of black marble; William Cope, Henry VII's cofferer, is buried there. In the churchyard are houses for chantry priests. A chapel dedicated to the Trinity stands in the middle of the town.

> At †the east end of the town is a bridge over the Cherwell; it has four fine stone arches.

Only one example of the good buildings that Leland saw survived the Civil War, Carpenter's shop at the west end of the market place, with half-timbering, gabled dormers and stuccoed plasterwork. Though the town did not greatly expand, much of it was rebuilt, only to be destroyed again by fire.

The spread of Oxford outside its medieval walls in the late sixteenth and early seventeenth century was due largely to an increase in the numbers of students. In the 1560s there were some three hundred entrants to the University, by the 1630s this had doubled. Five colleges were founded in this period; St John's 'to strengthen the orthodox faith' by Thomas White, Merchant Tailor of London, and Trinity, both in 1555, Jesus in 1571, Wadham in 1610 and Pembroke in 1624 by Thomas Tesdale, wool farmer at Glympton. In 1621 the earl of Danby gave the University the Physick Garden at the eastern end of the High Street while at the other end the Town Council erected a splendid fountain. Water brought from Hinksey in wooden pipes was fed into three cisterns, at Carfax, Christ Church, and outside All Saints church. One of the finest domestic buildings of this period is the Old Palace in St Aldate's. Then the residence of a merchant, it is elaborately decorated with plasterwork and carved woodwork.

Oxford was hardly typical of the area, though, in that they were freed from monastic control, many of the other towns could develop as the merchants themselves rather than the lord wished. A number of towns became the recipient of largesse in the form of buildings, some of them erected of necessity, some as a statement of wealth. Chipping Norton, for example, saw a new church tower, a guildhall, almshouses and a school built within a century, all provided by local men. On a lesser scale there was similar building activity at Bicester. Like Leland, we may speculate why Bicester, at least ten miles from all its nearest rivals, never developed into a major market centre, whereas Thame, the lands of its monastery bought by Lord Williams, prospered because of his enclosures and use of the lands for sheep farming. Subsidiary industries were established in the town, while suffering was alleviated by his almshouses. Its sons were educated in a grammar school established, also by Lord Williams, in 1559 and still part of the county's schools, and its market flourished. The finest part of the town, according to Leland, was in this area and it remained the wealthiest at the end of the seventeenth century.

Suffering and social requirements were not confined to towns. Rural poverty was real and, in days before easy transport, facilities few. Of necessity, men turned their minds, not without thought to their own lasting reputation, to filling the gaps in the social fabric left by the disappearance of monastic charity. The new men in a position to profit from the great sell-off saw, and seized, the opportunity offered by the cessation of monkish charity, especially in the distribution of alms to the poor and the provision of education, to blazon their wealth in new ways which ignored the church. The most conscientious built almshouses or schools, so that by the start of the Civil War even small villages could boast one or the other. Although Sutton Courtenay's school was held in a brick extension to the church porch, the schools at Williamscote, Bampton and Steeple Aston were in purpose-built buildings.

For those for whom building was beyond their means, there was always benefaction, its conditions writ large for all to see on a board displayed within the parish church. If this seemed too modest, even lesser men might bury themselves and their families contentedly beneath an elaborate tomb, for example, Sir William Barentyne at Great Haseley, Sir Michael Dormer at Great Milton, the Fermors at Somerton, Lady Unton at Faringdon and the Dixons at Little Rollright. The great men who lived within the county's bounds like William Pope at Wroxton, Sir Francis and Lady Knollys at Rotherfield Greys, Lord Chief Justice Tanfield at Burford and Dame Elizabeth Periam at Henley erected even more splendid monuments.

Building, benefaction or burial were, perhaps, the safest ways to keep in with both Man and God. Passions ran high over Henry VIII's abandonment of the church of Rome and the subsequent alterations to the liturgy. His decisions were not always accepted with the acquiescence of Thomas Holcott, whose memorial in Buckland church tells us he was first a lay preacher then, under Mary and the return to the Catholic church, prudently recanted, changing his mind yet again under Elizabeth. Unpleasantness was far more often the order of the day. In 1539 the Catholic Sir Adrian Fortescue of Stonor was beheaded for refusal to accept any change; ten years later the citizens of Chipping Norton witnessed the hanging of their rector from the church spire, though Bloxham's vicar, condemned to the same fate, seems to have won a reprieve. Not even the Reformation's ecclesiastical leaders escaped. The Martyrs' Memorial in Oxford was erected to king Henry's men, Archbishop Cranmer and bishops Latimer and Ridley, burned as heretics in the city in Mary's reign. 1549 saw a short-lived revolt, its causes a mixture of agrarian unrest and religious fervour, suppressed by a force of mercenaries and the hanging of ringleaders.

Prudence, as well as proclamation, dictated an end under the Tudors, to elaborate church building. Archbishop Cranmer's preface to the Book of Common Prayer makes it clear that the new form of worship was intended to be 'most easy and plain for the understanding of both the Readers and the Hearers ...' and 'commodious ... for the plainness of the order, and for that these Rules be few and easy'. Like the words, the church too had to be rearranged.

Statute commanded the destruction of frivolous imagery and decoration in line with the Protestant reaction to the decadence of Rome. Though it must remain uncertain how much was really destroyed between 1540 and the end of the century, images, carvings and glass, all easily and readily smashed, most certainly vanished. Whereas a cope from Steeple Aston is exhibited now at the Victoria & Albert Museum in London, church possessions sometimes passed into the possession of people who might have been considered more responsible. Thus at Middleton Stoney a cope was parcelled out amongst the church wardens; a cheap cup replaced the chalice which, together with a candlestick, had been sold for twelve pence. Some objects, however, have survived by accident; the brass lectern at Cropredy, thrown into the river and the alabaster altar reredos at Drayton, buried for safety. The bigger objects, such as the screens, often survived, even though mutilated in attempts to get rid of the offensive images, until Victorian restorers swept them away. The shrine of St Edburg of Bicester was taken from the Priory to the parish church at Stanton Harcourt where it may be seen today; fragments sufficient to allow reconstruction survived from similar shrines erected at Dorchester to St Birinus and in Oxford to St Frideswide. On the other hand, two shrines at Caversham were so thoroughly destroyed that when, less than two years later, the ever curious Leland passed by he did so without even discovering their existence.

Henry VIII's break with the Pope, his assumption of the headship of the Church of England and the dissolution of the monasteries did not denote a dramatic swing to the Protestant cause. Matters progressed a little further in the seven years of his son, only to be turned upside down in 1553 with the accession of his daughter Mary, who had never abandoned the Catholic faith. Her attempts, not the last, to reconcile England to Catholicism ended in failure. Mary's sister Elizabeth, queen from 1560, reverted cautiously to her father's 'reformed' church. These abrupt changes of direction were no inducement to spend one's wealth on beautifying a church. Bishop Jewel's porch, added to Sunningwell church in 1561, is an exception. Elizabeth's cautious establishment of a Protestant clergy, opposed to splendid ritual, discouraged any desire for large-scale alteration. Afraid of the strength of Puritan feeling, she forbade preaching so there was neither need nor reason to carve pulpits, reading desks or pews; the removal of the altar from the east end to the meeting point of chancel and nave, and the requirement that it should be a simple table, was an easy, if a dramatic, transformation. Many of these tables now stand near the entrance, displaying the church magazine or postcards. Elizabeth also ordered the display of the Royal Arms in a prominent position in the body of the church, stressing the connection between loyalty to the monarch and to the state church of which she was head. The board on which they were painted was usually hung over the chancel arch, newly whitewashed to obliterate all trace of its earlier mural. The custom continued through all subsequent reigns and several churches now display a long series.

Only with the accession of a new sovereign, James I, and the relaxation of some of the Elizabethan statutes, did a modicum of beauty return, demonstrated mostly in the woodwork required to fulfil the revived liturgical function of preaching. Pulpits and seating were needed again and fine examples are to be seen at Cumnor, Stanford in the Vale, East Hendred and Langford. The 1630s saw the building of two new churches, at Shrivenham by Lord Craven and at Besselsleigh by William Lenthall, the future Speaker of the House of Commons, examples rare in England.

While little attention was given to the church, more might be given to the parsonage; Rector Lydyat at Alkerton built himself a house with two ground floor rooms separated by a central fireplace and two sleeping chambers above. Rector Stubbings at Ambrosden, described as 'that jolly, fat doctor', spent £800 on a new residence; at Bletchingdon the rectory, repaired in 1637, consisted of hall, parlour and buttery with chambers above, kitchen, larder and dairy.

It was perhaps safer still not to push religion. The balance between those seeking more radical changes in doctrine and practice, the mass of those who attended church and those who sought to use the power of the church to bolster the power of the king was uneasy. In the 1630s Archbishop Laud ordered the altar to be moved back to the east end and to be railed round, reviving memories of Popish customs. His systematic visitations of every parish within his province to rout out divergence from Laudian practice, and to check on Catholic recusants and Puritan objectors alike, caused many to distrust him. His taste in ecclesiastical architecture, again reminiscent of Popish ways, went too far for many when he added the south porch with its twisting barley sugar pillars to the Oxford church of St Mary the Virgin. Archbishop Laud's disgrace and imprisonment formed part of the prelude to the outbreak of war, made inevitable when in January 1642 the king attempted to arrest five members of the House of Commons, amongst them John Hampden whose lands lay in Clare and Pyrton. It happens that the attempt was witnessed by yet another Oxfordshire man, the Speaker of the House, William Lenthall, born at Henley and owner of Besselsleigh and Burford Priory.

These men were two of a group which had for sometime been in the habit of living in each others' houses observing events and discussing what might be done to counter the king's only just legal measures to raise money without the help of parliament. One such meeting place was Broughton Castle, the property of the declared Puritan Lord Saye and Sele. The minds of this group were engaged not in conspiracy but in planning a constructive outcome to the impasse. Two measures had touched Oxfordshire deeply; the huge extension of the boundaries of Wychwood Forest and the revival of the medieval forest law which gave the king long forgotten jurisdiction over an area long since turned into farmland. There was also the levy known as Ship Money. Oxfordshire was required to supply a boat of 280 tons with a crew of one hundred and eighteen men or the sum of £3500; Berkshire was asked for £3400. Both measures were opposed; in the House of Commons Lenthall spoke out against the first and Hampden against the second. The county officers entrusted with raising Ship Money finally had to return the assessments in despair, declaring that many would not sign their names, amongst them the gentry of influence.

Like Elizabeth and James before him, Charles too had enjoyed the county's hospitality. His first visit in 1625 is remembered at Rycote Chapel by the splendid self-contained pew constructed especially for him. His third, in 1636, was perhaps the most splendid, its occasion being the opening of a new block of buildings at St John's College, its President Archbishop Laud. Amongst the entertainments, besides the performance of a masque, was a visit to the ingenious waterworks at Enstone, described for us by Dr Robert Plot, the county's first serious historian. A hermit rose from an urn to make a speech, followed first by a song from a rock answered by an echo and then by the all important banquet.

The Civil War was to put a permanent end to the king's pleasurable associations with the county; it was also to bring a temporary end to three generations of sustained prosperity. By 1642 the atmosphere had soured. For eleven years Charles had attempted to rule without parliament, just at the time when the class of person elected to the House of Commons was coming to realise that he was in a position to limit sovereign power by declining to vote taxes. The king's devices to fill his coffers without consulting the Commons – by selling offices, honours and trade monopolies and by reviving ancient, long discontinued royal rights – and Archbishop Laud's repressive religious policy produced resentment which was likely to end in an explosion. Even when the final break came, over a matter of parliamentary privilege, people were slow to take sides. A contemporary observed that 'the number of those who desired to sit still was greater than of those who desired to engage in either party'. In January the Speaker refused to divulge the whereabouts of five members of the House of Commons whom the king sought to arrest. Not until August did the king raised his standard in Nottingham.

The first serious engagement of the struggle was fought on Sunday 23 October almost by chance, at Edgehill, a little beyond the county's northwestern boundary. Neither side claimed victory. Inhabitants of nearby villages had no inkling of the event. Rector Harris of Hanwell observed that 'he took it for a great mercy that he heard not the least noise of the battel till the publick work of the day was over, nor could he believe the report of a fight till a soldier, besmeared with blood and powder, came to witness it'. Charles' troops straggled southwards attacking and briefly occupying Lord Say and Sele's castle at Broughton and making a more serious, and successful, attempt to seize his castle at Banbury, the first town to suffer pillage. The mayor's guarantee issued under the Royal seal that the town should not be plundered was pushed aside by Prince Rupert with the words 'My uncle little knowes what belongs to the warres'. The town surrendered after three days. The castle was held by Royalists for the next four years.

Less than a week later Charles came to rest at Oxford. The establishment of his headquarters there inevitably associated the area closely with the struggle which followed. Because of its central location within England the county saw a lot of activity, though virtually no serious action. Only two minor engagements took place within its boundaries, the battles of Chalgrove Field and Cropredy Bridge.

At Oxford Charles was welcomed by members of the University, affronted by Lord Saye and Sele's brief occupation and search for college silver and plate. Although the townsmen did not share this enthusiasm, the place was a comfortable and convenient shelter for the Court, if not a practical centre for one whose forces came largely from the north and west of England. The king resided at Christ Church, the queen was installed at Merton. The Royal Mint, in New Inn Hall street, issued Oxford Crowns with the inscription 'The Protestant Religion, the Laws of England, the Liberties of Parliament', while Oseney Mill was turned over to the production of gunpowder. Elaborate fortifications, designed against artillery, were constructed far outside the medieval line of the walls with the unwilling help of the townsmen. Life at Court continued in Oxford almost as normal.

Royalists also commanded Wallingford Castle, held by Governor Blagge. Prince Rupert's cavalry was quartered at Abingdon. Oxford was ringed by garrisons billeted on the wealthy owners of large houses; Islip, Bletchingdon, Woodstock, Godstow and Gaunt House, a network within which Charles must, at first, have felt reasonably secure. Outposts were held to the west at Faringdon House by Sir Marmaduke Rawdon and to the southeast at Shirburn and Mapledurham. The two last were close to the parliamentary towns of Thame, Chinnor and Henley where Phyllis Court was fortified and Fawley Court counter-balanced royalist Greenlands. Other parliamentary strongholds, such as Aylesbury and wavering Bicester, Broughton Castle and Newbury, must have seemed satisfactorily far away.

Early in 1643 the royalists won a skirmish at Burford, only to lose the city of Reading in April, taken from them by forces commanded by the earl of Essex and John Hampden. A parliamentary detachment moved northwards and the earl set up his headquarters at Thame, his rear protected by outposts at Chinnor, Bledlow, Stokenchurch and Wycombe. He attacked Islip, but was repulsed. Prince Rupert rode out from Oxford and attacked the troops holding Postcombe; having overpowered them Rupert continued to Chinnor. He attacked, killing fifty men and capturing one hundred and twenty prisoners. He then set fire to the village and prepared to return to Oxford, choosing, of the two routes open to him, to come via Chalgrove and cross the river Thame over Leland's 'timber bridge supported on five stone pillars' at Chiselhampton rather than via Wheatley. Hampden, at Watlington, requested troops from the earl, going himself to hold the bridge. Rupert was victorious, Hampden retiring from the field with a bullet in his shoulder. He died six days later at an inn in Thame.

Essex withdrew to Aylesbury, a retreat which permitted a large convoy of arms and ammunition, and the queen herself, to arrive in Oxford. The next battle, the first fought at Newbury was inconclusive in military terms, but the king's loss in personal terms because of the deaths of three commanders. One had had an Oxfordshire connection – Lucius Cary, Viscount Falkland, grandson of Sir Lawrence Tanfield builder of Burford Priory, and owner of an estate at Great Tew, Secretary of State to the king. His body was brought back to Great Tew and buried by night.

By the end of 1643 the king was in the stronger position, with ports open to him in the west, his line of outposts ringing Oxford intact. The parliamentarians revised their strategy, dividing their forces into two armies, in order to diminish the king's advantage. Royalist forces had either to divide, or come together in greater numbers, concentrated over a smaller area. Charles chose the latter, withdrawing into Oxford and abandoning even Wallingford and Abingdon. The latter was immediately occupied by Essex, whose forces succeeded in crossing the Thames at Sandford Ferry and marched to headquarters at Islip. The king decided to attack Sir William Waller, parliament's second commander, at Abingdon. Waller, however, succeeded in crossing at Newbridge and reaching Eynsham, from where there should have been little difficulty in joining up with Essex at Islip. To prevent this, Charles directed a diversionary attack to be made on Abingdon to distract attention from his own bold move as he left the city across Port Meadow to reach Burford by way of Wolvercote, Yarnton and Hanborough. Pursued by only one parliamentary general and his troops, Charles made a circuit through Worcester, Bewdley and Bridgnorth before doubling back to Burford, rejoining the main body of his army. The king

then made for Banbury by way of Bicester. Foiled in his plan to take possession of Crouch Hill west of the town, because it took too long for his forces
to pass in single file over Banbury's bridge, Charles continued northwards
up the east bank of the Cherwell. Waller kept pace on the west bank. Battle,
joined at Cropredy Bridge on 29 June 1644, left Waller the loser and the
king free to engage the earl of Essex in the west.

The outcome did, however, make parliament decide to put an end to the
royalist occupation of Banbury castle. For three months, from July to
October 1644, the castle was bombarded by the parliamentary army from
batteries placed near the church, at the North Bar and in the Market Place.
All they achieved was to breach the western wall over a length of thirty
yards (27m). Plans to mine the walls elsewhere failed when tunnelling
released hidden springs of water. Even an attempt to scale the walls by first
filling the ditches with bundles of furze was unsuccessful. The siege came
to an end when royalist reinforcements were sent from Oxford. The
besiegers retired, allowing the castle's governor his first sleep in three
months!

Military action intensified in 1645. Speaker Lenthall's house at
Besselsleigh, occupied by royalist forces at the end of the previous year,
was recaptured by parliamentary troops who then burnt it to the ground to
prevent its recapture. Cromwell was sent into the county to distract the
king from his preparations for further campaigns. One by one the garrisons
which encircled Oxford were overcome. Advancing through Watlington
and Wheatley, Cromwell learned that royalist forces held the bridge at Islip;
they were chased to Bletchingdon where they found refuge with the garrison commanded by Colonel Windebank in the house of the former sheriff,
Sir Thomas Coghill. Cromwell demanded its surrender; to his relief, it did.
He wrote afterwards that he had had doubts about a successful storming,
'for it is strong and well defended'. Its commander was court-martialled
and shot, for cowardice, by his own side.

Cromwell moved on westwards, heading towards royalist Faringdon
already under attack. On the way he laid siege to Godstow House which
surrendered on 23 May only after the outhouses had been fired, to Gaunt
House, the property of Samuel Fell, dean of Christ Church, which guarded
the Thames crossing at Newbridge, and to the minor fort at Radcot Bridge.
At Bampton he routed forces under Colonel Vaughan. Meanwhile Charles
marched out of Oxford on 6 May towards Worcester. By 22 May Cromwell
had set up his headquarters at Marston and the city was under siege. It was
raised two weeks later to free the troops for the battle of Naseby. When
Charles returned to Oxford in August it was with only a handful of sur-

vivors. All over the country his strongholds were falling to parliamentary forces, amongst them Faringdon House. In February 1646 Banbury castle was again under siege; it surrendered on hearing the news that the king had sought refuge with the Scots at Newark, who subsequently sold him to his enemies.

At the start of hostilities some few gentlemen had hastened to put their houses into a defensible state. Robert Dormer at Rousham drilled holes in his front door large enough for muskets to poke through from within; at Ditchley earthworks were dug in the park. At Phyllis Court, the property of Bulstrode Whitelocke, a supporter of Cromwell, more extensive preparations were made. We know of them only as they were destroyed at the end of the fighting.

> I had a great number of countrymen, my neighbours, who willingly came in to me upon my warrant with mattocks, shovels and some carts to help in the slighting of the works ... In a few days, having many hands, I threw in the breastworks on two sides and made two even side walks, the one on the side next the Thames, the other on the North side. On the two other sides I caused the bulwarks and lines to be digged down, the grafts (moats) filled, the drawbridge to be pulled up and all levelled. I sent away the great guns, the granadoes, fireworks and ammunition, whereof there was good store in the fort.

Grandiose precautions of this sort had not been a great deal of use. People had been far more inconvenienced by hungry soldiers searching for food than by direct attack. At Little Rollright Cecilia Dixon was still lying-in after childbirth when soldiers quartered themselves in her house, demanding that she rise and look after them in proper style. The rector of Alkerton, Thomas Lydyat, Fellow of New College, builder of the rectory, had his home pillaged four times. He himself, for denying money to the soldiers and defending his books and papers, was twice carried from his rectory and 'infamously used' by the soldiers. His losses were so great that eventually he had to borrow a shirt for three months. He could count himself lucky; another priest, Dr Oldys, rector of Adderbury, was shot in the back by a Roundhead horseman. An Epwell man and his wife, who described themselves as poor and aged, were held prisoner in their own house for a week during which soldiers violently took away most of their household goods. In their petition for compensation they claimed loss of money and of 'seven pairs of sheets, three brass kettles, pewter, clothing, candles, eggs, bowls and spoons'.

Charles in captivity was allowed to spend time with his children at Caversham in the house of Lord Craven. From the same house Charles was in the habit of walking to an inn with a bowling green at Collins End nearby. Not everyone wished to be seen in his company, however. Bulstrode Whitelocke, hearing that the king intended to visit him at Phyllis Court, invented business in London and left his house at His Majesty's disposal. The execution of the king marked the end of the struggle. There was a brief attempt to restore his son, made in 1651. A possibly apocryphal story is told of Arthur Jones, owner of Chastleton. Returning from the battle of Worcester at which the Royalists were defeated, he was followed by a troop of Roundheads believing him to be the fleeing Charles II. Arthur hid in a secret room over the porch. His indomitable wife Sarah laced the soldiers' beer with opium from her medicine chest. As they slept, he rode off on one of their best horses. In all probabilty he was able to escape abroad, avoiding all the many changes which took place during the rule of parliament under Cromwell.

Commonwealth, Restoration and Commemoration 1649-1714

Traces of the damage inflicted on the fabric of buildings during the fighting in the Civil War are still to be seen; cannon ball lodged in Faringdon's church tower which lost its spire, the broken crosses at East Hagbourne, a brass scored by shot in the church at Newnham Murren near Wallingford, the names of captives carved on the pulpit in St John's church Burford, cannon balls in Cropredy church supposed to have been taken from the battlefield. However, the war was more disruptive than destructive; the passage of armies, the need to supply food for men and fodder for horses, to feed the royalist headquarters established at Oxford and the garrisons quartered nearby, together with the general uncertainty about the outcome and the effects on trade, put an end to initiatives in peaceful fields.

The aftermath of the fighting is revealed in various forms. It is a measure of the strength of the royal cause in Oxfordshire that at least one parliamentarian, Captain Abercrombie, vowed 'to make Oxfordshire so poor that even the school children should curse him'. He did not get his way, but the consequences of the war for some of the monarchy's most loyal supporters were often serious. Some of those whose property had already suffered destruction now had to face confiscation of their estates or heavy fines. Sir John Fettiplace of Childrey paid £1943. Sir Thomas Coghill of Bletchingdon, whose house had been attacked, entered into voluntary imprisonment for debt in an attempt to avoid further harassment. Sir Thomas Brooks of North Aston protected his estates for a time by leasing them to friends and relatives before being forced to sell to a parliamentarian speculator in forfeited lands.

Houses which had been destroyed, either by their owners or by the forces of their opponents, were sometimes sold and sometimes left standing ruinous, a grim reminder of what had passed. Thus Godstow and Woodstock were never rebuilt; the bishop of Oxford's new palace at Cuddesdon was not reconstructed until 1679. Two gate piers are all that remain of Speaker Lenthall's twice sacked house at Besselsleigh. Fawley Court, sacked by the royalists, remained ruinous for some twenty years, while at neighbouring Phyllis Court a certain amount of rebuilding was put in hand immediately. For a few, the end of the war became a source of profit. Lord Saye and Sele, for example, was paid compensation for the destruction of his castle of Banbury. A purchaser was found for the slighted castle of Wallingford and the parliamentary Commissioners reporting on the state of the palace at Woodstock deemed the buildings better worthy to stand than to be demolished. They were sold for rather more than £20,000. If Sir Robert Cecil was correct in writing in 1604 that 'The place is unwholesome, all the house standing upon springs. It is unsavoury, for there is no savour but of cows and pigs. It is uneaseful, for only the King and Queen ... are lodged in the house' this, together with the pounding it took before surrendering in 1646, suggests that it was no great loss to the Crown and no gain to the new owner.

The clergy were also amongst those to suffer. The defeat of the royalist forces gave the strongly Puritan elements in the parliamentarian army the upper hand in ecclesiastical affairs. One of their first measures was to eject strongly royalist or staunchly Anglican clergy and to replace them by men with more Puritan leanings. Some twenty-eight parsons in Oxfordshire were ejected; few of them ever received the pensions arranged from them. Thus the vicar of Sandford and Iffley was reduced to earning his living by working as a wood-cutter, while his wife worked for the tailor who let them lodgings. The 'name, title and dignity' of the bishop of Oxford was 'wholly abolished and taken away', but this did not stop him from continuing to ordain new priests in his out of the way rectory at Launton. Churches, often used during the fighting as prisons, hospitals, gunpowder stores, stables or barracks, again suffered destruction of their fittings. In 1659 the Oxford gossip, Anthony Wood, walked from Oxford to Banbury and reported that he saw little of the heraldic glass he knew had been in the windows before.

The execution of king Charles I, his death warrant signed by at least one Oxfordshire man, Henry Marten of Longworth, was followed by the assumption of power by a body of men without experience of government, held precariously together by strong, but discordant religious beliefs and ill-formed notions of their own power. Uneasy peace settled only slowly and some things had changed for ever. The building boom was in suspense. It was only partly because farmers were no longer making the enormous profits they had enjoyed for the two previous generations; surviving wills show that the levels of personal wealth achieved by 1640 remained stable, though they did not increase. More significantly, many potential patrons were travelling abroad, some on their own, others attached to the court circle.

One such man was Sir Roger Pratt, who had left England in 1645 on an architectural tour of France and the Netherlands. Already inclined towards architecture he used his time to observe the fashions of the Continent, much more deeply influenced by the Italian Palladio than England had yet been. On his return his cousin, another Roger Pratt, commissioned him to build a new country house, sited at Coleshill. Its design was revolutionary, the first major rethink of the implications, and possibilities, of living on more than one level. In the words of Celia Fiennes, who visited it some forty years later, it was

> filled with all sorts of things improved for pleasure and use; the house is new built with stone, most of the offices are partly underground – kitchen, pantry, butlery and good cellars – and round a court is all the other offices and outhouses; these are all even with the back yards. The entrance of the house is an ascent of severall steps into a hall so lofty the roof is three storeys...

Having described in detail the arrangement of the rooms, she then described the great staircase 'spacious and handsome', put in place in 1662, some ten years after the start of building. Placed in the centre of the house, with two separate branches ascending to a gallery running the whole length of the hall, Coleshill was one of the first houses so to position the stair instead of placing it in the corner of a room or a turret. The decision radically changed the status of the stair. Burnt down in 1952 the ground plan is now laid out in flowers in the Clock House garden, beyond the original gateposts standing beside the B4013.

Few other buildings, even on a small scale, are known to date from the 1650s, the time of Cromwell's rule. The manor house at Nether Worton, now much altered, bears a date stone of 1653, and College Farm, South Newington, is dated to 1659. The Restoration and return of king Charles II in 1660 marked a construction boom, this time in the hands of the seriously wealthy and influential. Three important houses were sited in the Vale; Ashdown House, Milton Manor and Kingston Bagpuize. A less certainly dated fourth was built at Kingston Lisle. Ashdown, built for the earl of Craven in the 1660s, is constructed of chalk blocks with grey Bath stone dressings. Tall and square, topped by a cupola with a golden ball, it looks like a doll's house, standing at the meeting place of four avenues. Remarkably similar in plan, though not in appearance, is the core of brick-built Milton Manor, complete by 1663. The original plans still exist. Front and rear facades are identical, their five bays divided by Ionic pilasters topped by festooned stone capitals. Also of brick and with identical frontages, Kingston Bagpuize, where Charles I had spent a night during the

Newbury campaign in the Tudor manor, was probably also built at this time. None was as advanced as Coleshill, but each nevertheless made a feature of the newfangled staircase. At Ashdown and Milton it occupied one corner of a square structure, flight turning on flight to rise through three floors. At Kingston Bagpuize it was placed in a separate hall behind the main entrance; it climbed on three walls, supported by only one post, to end in a gallery which gave access to the principal rooms. A separate stair ran from basement to attic. It is clear that the owners of all these houses had both taste and money sufficient to command the best workmen and, though we do not know their names, the best architects. Other, smaller-scale houses were erected. Of Ascott House near Stadhampton, only the gatepiers still remain beside the B480. Adderbury House was remodelled by the wife of the dissolute Lord Rochester while her husband disported himself at Court. Kiddington Hall was built slightly later.

The staircase became the visible and feted novelty. The other relatively new feature, the fireplace or hearth, became an object of taxation, first in 1662 and again in 1665. The returns suggest a widespread degree of comfort. In addition to listing the hearths in each house in the village, those excused from payment, on grounds of poverty, are also named. The rate in Oxfordshire was low, some 11%. In the Vale it was almost three times as high.

Townsmen too could afford a display of wealth. Faringdon, Watlington and Wallingford each acquired a town hall. The most magnificent was built at Abingdon by Christopher Kempster, whose family was one of those owning quarries at Taynton. Described in a testimonial by Sir Christopher Wren as 'discreet and honest', Kempster's work, considered by Celia Fiennes to be the finest example in England, still dominates the market square. He was a member of one of the new kind of families which now plentiful documentation allows us to trace. The reverse of those we have dealt with earlier, where London merchants bought into the country, Kempster's family wealth derived from quarries at Little Barrington and Taynton. Supplying stone, much in demand not only for the rebuilding of London after the Fire of 1666, but also for the country houses being built throughout England, brought Kempster as contracting mason into contact with many of the growing number of architects. His cottage, on the outskirts of Burford, is a surprisingly modest dwelling for one so quietly successful. Another Taynton family were the Strongs, whose members were associated in various capacities with buildings in the area, as were the Townesends of Oxford.

Belonging to a different, but not dissimilar, group, was the Quaker Early family, blanket manufacturers at Witney. Witney blankets were already famous by the time it is possible to trace the family's rise to pre-eminence amongst several weaving families in the town. Apprenticed to a Quaker blanket-maker by his father, also a weaver, Thomas Early inherited his childless master's business. In 1688 he was chosen to make and present two gold-fringed blankets to King James II on a visit to Woodstock. The blanket industry was recovering from a brief recession. Witney's chief weavers had petitioned the Lord Chancellor for help in 1669-70, calling his attention to 'the low condition of this poore town which hath heretoforth bin a place of great trading and hath yielded much reliefe not only to the poore Inhabitants, but to the working poor about it'. The aim of the petitioners was 'to bring the town into a condition where its people might be able to live most prosperously and comfortably within themselves without being a trouble and burthen in craving and receiving assistance from theyr neighbours'. None of their suggestions was adopted for another forty-one years.

The life style of such people is illustrated in the will of another such moderately prosperous man, Alexander Calcott, a baker in Hook Norton, who died in December 1682 leaving goods and cash to the value of £72 15s. He lived in a six-roomed house, reasonably comfortably furnished. Its hub was still the hall, where cooking and eating took place; to one side lay the parlour, to the other the back parlour. Above were three bedrooms, while the yard outside contained the bakehouse and a store. His daughter received most of the best articles, presumably to ensure that she was provided with a good dowry. They included Alexander's spice mortar and pestle, his best brass pottage pot, three pewter platters and three dishes with Margaret's name on them, his great carved chest and all the furniture in the room above the parlour. The living standards of his wife, appointed his sole executrix, were little disturbed by this arrangement; his sister was to receive twenty shillings within a year of his death. The inventory, made by his brother and his sister's husband, is worth quoting in some detail.

In the chamber over the parlour one joined bedstead, one featherbed, one straw bed, under it one feather bolster, one feather pillow and set of scarlet curtains and valance to the same, one red rug, one red counterpane, one pair of blankets, two pairs of sheets £6

And in the same room, one oval table and frame, eight red leather chairs, four pictures, one little pair of dogs, one fire shovel and one pair of fire tongs £2

In the chamber over the hall one joined bedstead, one truckle bed, one feather bed, one set of curtains and other furniture belonging to the said bed, one table and frame, one great chest and some other implements in that room £3

In the chamber over the backhouse, one bedstead, one flock bed with the furniture thereunto belonging, five old coffers, two boxes, one bolting mill and other lumber and other implements in that room £2 10s.6d.

Three pairs of sheets, two table cloths, one dozen napkins, two pillow beers and all other small linen £1 10s.0d.

In the parlour one table and frame, one court cupboard, five chairs and two joined stools £1

In the backhouse one furnace, one dough trough, two moulding boards and other tools of trade £4

In the cellar, six barrels, two yeilling vats and other brewing vessels, and two dozen of hemp £2

Two dozen glass bottles 2s.

In the hall, one table and frame, one cupboard, two forms, one screen, one bacon rack, one pair of andirons and other fire irons, one woollen wheel, one linen wheel, one flitch and a half of bacon and two shelves £2

Three kettles, three pottage pots, two posnets, one warming pan, two spits and two tin pans £1 10s. 0d.

Also ten pewter platters, eight flagons, four pewter candlesticks, four pewter plates, two chamber pots, six porringers and other small pewter ware and two dozen trenchers £2

Also, in the stable fuel house and outside, 500 bundles of furze, one log, one hogwash stone and all other wood implements and lumber about the backside and inside not before named £3

His house was typical of the many three and four hearth properties listed for the hearth tax and to be seen all over the county. His lifestyle was comfortable, though not grand, neither his property nor his furnishings bearing any comparison with those of the big houses and not much to those of the clergy. With the reestablishment of the Anglican church clerics showed an interest in building, for themselves if not for the church itself. Considerable attention might be given to the erection of parsonage houses, some of which were extremely comfortable, as at Stanton Harcourt (1677), Islip (1689) and Buscot (1705). The clergy, often the younger sons of noble or at least well-to-do families, had a firm belief in their right to a standard of living equal to that of their brothers and well-married sisters. Neither the clergy nor their patrons gave the same attention to the church. At best the building might be embellished by memorials or slabs, the finest those of the once disgraced Fettiplace family at Swinbrook.

The war had some surprising effects on the balance between differing religious sects. The composition of Cromwell's armies encouraged the nonconformists (those who refused to conform to the Church of England) to come into the open, which they did easily under the Commonwealth and, though not at first freely, with fewer and fewer difficulties after the Restoration, in particular the Baptists and the Quakers. Baptist congregations are known in the Vale, organised by the Cornishman John Pendarves, from 1648 at Wantage, Abingdon by 1652, Longworth by 1656 and Faringdon by 1657. After the Restoration prosecutions of Baptists at Abingdon Borough Sessions were frequent. After the relaxation of the penal laws in 1672 it became easier to get a licence to preach and consequently very much easier to hold meetings in the open. It was also less dangerous to keep records of births, marriages and deaths. By the end of the 1670s there was a regional Baptist association based on Abingdon, drawing its members from the towns of the Vale.

The Berkshire Quarterly Meeting of the Quakers was established in 1668. The principal centres of Quaker activity lay outside the area, but Abingdon, Appleton, Blewbury, Faringdon and Uffington all had members. The latter held meetings near Garrards Farm. A separate Meeting was established north of the Thames, also in 1668, with Meetings at Oxford, Banbury and Warborough.

But if the organisational and administrative aspects of nonconformity might be relatively easy to put in place, groups were still small and poor. Though many of their preachers had been officers in the parliamentary armies, the established Church had little to fear from the social standing of most nonconformists. Few squires were counted amongst the dissenters; Mr Blake of Cogges was one. Another, Bray Doyly, was treated leniently by magistrates because of his social standing. A memorial to a third is in Shrivenham church; the Anabaptist John Wildman who died in 1693 as Sir John directed in his will that

> if his executors should think fit, there should be some stone of small price set near his ashes, to signify, without foolish flattery, to his posterity, that in that age lived a man who spent the best part of his days in prisons, without crimes, being conscious of no offence towards man, for that he so loved his God that he could serve no man's will and wished the liberty and happiness of his country and of all mankind.

His son's memorial states that 'he preferred confinement for many years with his father, who was a prisoner in the Isle of Scilly, in the reign of Charles II, to the full enjoyment of his liberty'. Congregations, however, were mainly made up of working men, and it was not until the next century that their descendants could afford to erect the first buildings.

The Catholics, on the other hand, included many of the old-established families, who still lived in the houses that had been theirs for generations using the surviving medieval chapel for their own rites. Stonor, Mapledurham, Heythrop, Tusmore Park, Britwell Prior, Sandford on Thames, Great Haseley, Overy near Dorchester, Waterperry, Buckland, East Hendred and Lyford Grange were all Catholic centres. Their congregations too might come from far afield but, discreetly practising, they were rarely prosecuted. Very slowly the link between dissent or non-attendance at Anglican services and the fear of civil disobedience was dissolving, though real tolerance lay far in the future.

The gossiping Anthony Wood of Oxford and the ever-inquisitive Dr Plot, whose *Natural History of Oxfordshire* was first published in 1677, are together Oxfordshire's equivalent of London's Samuel Pepys. Plot's list of gentleman's residences includes the properties of several of the king's ministers. He reveals also their preoccupations, giving us a glimpse of the concerns and interests of the landed gentry in his descriptions of the new models of farm carts and waggons, the methods of aerating ricks, and in his discussions of mills and their various ingenious uses. One at Hanwell both ground corn and cut stone, while another could be used to drill the boreholes in guns; the most elaborate was that of the Fermor family at Tusmore, operated by one horse and a man carried round 'in a sort of coach-box behind the horse'. This mill could grind apples for cider, cut wheat in four different finenesses, cut and winnow oats and produce oatmeal and 'lastly it makes mustard which indeed is a mere curiosity. And all these it performs severally or together, according as is desired'.

Plot discloses to us the gentleman's interest in farming and in the improvement of yields from his land. Experiments were made with new crops such as pulses and sainfoin, literally 'the healthy herb' used for winter fodder, with machines and with rotation patterns. One of the earliest and most renowned of the experimenters was Jethro Tull who lived for a time at Howbery Court, near Wallingford, where he invented – and perfected his drill in 1701. Thwarted by his labourers' dislike of his passion for new methods, he resolved 'to contrive an engine to plant St Foin (sainfoin) more faithfully than such hands would do'. Alongside technical developments were changes in the manner of using the land. The older two-field

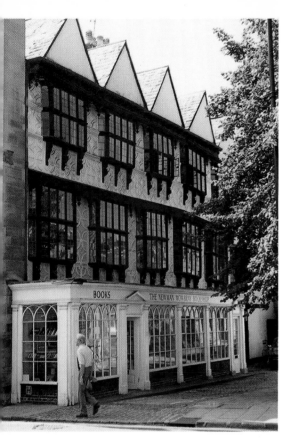

Left: The Old Palace, Oxford

Below right: The Almshouses, Steeple Aston

Below left: Milton Manor

Above left: Wroxton, fingerpost

Above: Faringdon Market Hall

Below left: Witney, Blanketmaker's Hall

Below: Judge Page's tomb, Steeple Aston

system was often altered into a four-field system, known as 'Quarters', so that more land might be taken into cultivation rather than lying fallow to recover. Such trials were usually the prelude to more intensive farming and thus to the smaller fields of enclosed land. Although there are cases of enclosure by agreement, particularly in small townships with few freehold-ers or where the terrain was suited to grazing or in the old forest town-ships, only about 13% of the county was enclosed by the end of the century.

Another sign of change to come is contained in the plan to develop navi-gation on the Thames. Already improved by pound locks to regularise the water flow, an ex-army landowning captain, Andrew Yarranton, suggested in 1677 that the river should be joined to the Avon from Lechlade and thus to the Severn, while the Cherwell should be made navigable to Banbury. The prime reason for undertaking this labour was to halve the cost of carry-ing goods from the north and west to London; the second was because 'these waterways will carry corn and malt from Banbury and thereabouts to be sent to London, Banbury and near it being the only fruitful place for goodness and quantities of corn in England'. Neither scheme materialised. Celia Fiennes saw the river between Abingdon and Oxford 'full of barges and lighters' and Kempster sent his stone to Radcot and thence down-stream to London.

The river might suit the transport of heavy loads, but travellers were becoming used to the much quicker road communications. The first of the flying coaches ran between Oxford and London in 1671, when it was adver-tised that

> every day in the week there will be a coach set out (at six o'clock in the morning) from Thomas Moor's house over against All Souls Colledge which shall com-modiously perform the whole journey to London in one day and from the Saracen's Head on Snow Hill, London to Oxford again the next day, and so con-stantly for this summer half year. *If God Permit*

The erection of a stone signpost at Wroxton, decorated with pointing fin-gers, by Francis White in 1686 confirms the increase in road traffic, and the beginning of its special needs. Coaches made Oxford's links to London eas-ier, but while the city was still an occasional venue for Parliament, royalty's link with the county were no longer close. The royal residences had passed into private hands. Only one would be remembered when, in 1704, it was decided to commemorate the victories of the Duke of Marlborough over the French armies of Louis XIV at Blenheim on the Danube. The fitting monu-ment was to be a palace, within the royal park at Woodstock, presented as a gift to the Duke by Queen Anne. Funds too were made available and building began in a blaze of enthusiasm. The architect, John Vanbrugh, found, on canvassing opinion, that everyone thought that although the building was to be a private habitation

> yet it ought, at the same time, to be considered both as a Royal and a National Monument and care taken with the design, and the execution, that it might have the qualitys proper to such a monument, namely Beauty, Magnificence and Duration.

Work began in June 1705, carried out by the finest craftsmen of the day. They included the quarry-owning Strongs of Taynton, father and son, Henry Banckes another local quarry owner, the Oxford Peisleys and William Townesend as carpenters; later, Grinling Gibbons executed the interior carvings and Sir James Thornhill the paintings. Nicholas Hawksmoor, clerk to Sir Christopher Wren, supervised from afar while Vanbrugh lived for a while in the now really ruinous old palace. His wish that this should remain standing as a focal point for the new gardens was over-ruled by the duchess who, in turn, was over-ruled in the final choice of design. Queen Anne herself approved Vanbrugh's model, of a central block standing separate from, but connected to, projecting wings.

By 1712, when funds were cut off by a change in government, only a skeleton building, much of it unfinished inside, had been achieved. The star team of workmen packed up and dispersed. When work resumed in 1716 it was pushed ahead by the duchess, afraid that her sick husband would die before completion and that the palace would become a memorial to a dead man. By 1719 they were able to move into a still unfinished building.

The gardens, the Great Parterre, the kitchen and the duchess's flower garden, begun at the same time as the structure and the stuff of the duke's dreams while again on campaign, fared better. It is reported that the duke himself had begged the royal gardener to consider that

> he was an old man and could not expect to live until the trees were grown up and expected, as it were, to have a garden ready for him. Accordingly Mr Wise transplanted thither full grown trees in baskets, which he buried in the earth, which look and thrive the same as if they had stood there thirty or forty years.

These gardens were destroyed and laid out again later in the century by Capability Brown at the same time and in the same spirit as Horace Walpole observed of the building 'execrable within, without and almost all round'.

Georgian and Regency 1714-1832

Vanbrugh's efforts at Blenheim, unappreciated by the duchess, and by no means meeting with universal approval, nevertheless spurred others into action. The area saw an explosion of building activity, at the rate of at least one major house each decade. None rivalled Blenheim for size, but on a lesser, though still considerable, scale the residences at Ditchley, Cornbury and Heythrop were enlarged. On a more intimate scale houses sprang up all over the area. Many of the smaller houses were entirely new, amongst them Buscot, Buckland, Chiselhampton and Ardington. Here Edward Clarke borrowed money from his neighbour at West Lockinge, a successful speculator in the South Sea Bubble, to build a new house around 1721. It was concealed from the village by a screen of trees and set in a small park sloping to Lockinge brook. Built in three different kinds of brick, the exactly symmetrical house may have been designed by Thomas Strong, of the quarry-owning family of Taynton. The entrance and the garden facades were identical, as were the side elevations. The interior seems to have been as carefully planned, the arrangement of rooms on each of four floors being much the same. Open corridors ran through the house, remaining still on the attic and the basement floors. Ardington's greatest feature, however, was the unusual staircase which occupies much of the entrance hall. Two flights rise along the walls on either side of the garden entrance, meeting at a half landing and then merging into a single flight to reach the cross gallery.

The work bankrupted Clarke; even the demolition and sale of the two houses his bride brought him did nothing to ease the financial situation. Clarke sold most of his estate to the neighbour at Lockinge who had first underwritten the undertaking, and himself struggled on with barely sufficient land to meet his expenses.

His seem to have been exceptional circumstances. Some families built their residences several times over on the same site; the Fermors at Tusmore, for example, and the Annesleys at Bletchingdon. At Glympton Sir Thomas Wheate requested, and received, plans from Sir John Vanbrugh around 1709 as a reward for having supplied stone from quarries on his land for the building of Blenheim. They were never executed; an inferior design was carried out in the 1740s. Greater extravagance still is demonstrated in the activities of the Turners of Ambrosden who had no sooner erected their house and employed Capability Brown, the country's most famous gardener, to landscape the garden than, dissatisfied, they had it pulled it down.

The ultimate in the restless energy that characterises the period is demonstrated by the wandering Harcourts. Sometime after the Restoration they abandoned the old manor house at Stanton Harcourt for a newly-built up-to-date residence at Cokethorpe Park, now a school. Some fifty years later, swayed by new fashions, they moved to their other property at Nuneham Courtenay where they built another completely new house, parts of it using stone brought from the old manor. Lady Harcourt described their plans to her son as

> a design we have of building a villa ... not a seat, as was talked of; for beside the immense sum such a thing would cost, there is absolutely not a spot upon the whole estate ... so proper for a house as near the clump of elms, which you are sensible, cannot contain a large building. However, I think the situation will make amends for the smallness of the building.

Modest though the plan may sound, the construction of the house in fact required the shifting of the village, not only because it would be in full view of the big house, but also because it occupied the most scenic site above the Thames. A visitor some forty years later described the process, remarkable in that it was achieved within twelve months.

> The village was originally in the Park at no great distance from the House and consisted of pretty, white cottages, scattered around a small piece of water and shaded with a number of very fine trees. The late Lord Harcourt, thinking the village too near the house, built a new one on the Oxford road, about a mile from the mansion house. But the poor people were very unwilling to leave their old habitation and several houses in the New Village remained for a long time uninhabited ... One poor old woman known by the name of Babs whose cottage was shaded by a tree of her own planting in a most beautiful situation begged she might be permitted to remain there during the remainder of her life. She was indulged in this request and died there.

The reconstructed village, laid out along the newly-made turnpike, is still to be seen on the present A4070. For years it remained without a church for, though the village had been unsightly and its Gothic church an offence to good taste, that same building, remodelled as a Grecian temple, was just what Earl Harcourt desired. The villagers, much to their disgust, were required to worship in it until, at the end of the nineteenth century, a church was erected closer to their homes.

The removal of the village formed the subject of Goldsmith's poem *The Deserted Village*. The remodelling of the gardens by the fashionable landscape gardener Capability Brown, was the subject of much cogitation, many alterations, and the inspiration for another set of verses.

> We laundry maids at Nuneham
> Are the happiest maids in the nation
> With a rub, rub, rub and a frothing tub,
> And a charming situation
>
> No more shall our caps and aprons
> Be torn by gooseberry bushes
> Or our ruffles be rent by the thistle and bent,
> Or our sheets be soil'd with rushes.
>
> Our lines shall grace laburnums,
> Since our master's will is,
> And our smaller things shall dangle on strings
> From tuberose tops and lilies.
>
> No more in our chests of linen
> Shall lavender reign despotic.
> We'll cull our flowers from yonder bowers
> And our smocks shall smell exotic.

If the scansion of these verses leaves something to be desired, the idea underlying them is clear enough. Lord and villager no longer needed each other for protection. The lines of social demarcation had been drawn and neither village nor villagers could be permitted to blight the vista. The great house, symbol of wealth and authority, was to stand in isolation, and in its own artificial landscape, for it was in the eighteenth century that man first began to mould Nature to an unalarming tameness.

The obsession with the scenic is perhaps best seen at Rousham where, in the 1730s, William Kent enlarged the Tudor and Jacobean house, adding a library and prettifying the interior. The Painted Parlour, for which he designed furniture, carved wall brackets and painted the ceiling, shows him at his best. He then built the stables, perhaps as a practice run for his work at the Horse Guards Parade which it closely resembles. Finally, Kent turned his attention to the gardens, designing a series of walks and vistas, pools, ponds and temples. They were intended to be viewed in a particular sequence, starting from the newly laid out bowling green on the north front of the house. His efforts to conquer Nature extended beyond the park; he incorporated the medieval bridge into the background of a water garden and, on the banks of the River Cherwell, he erected a new mill designed to look like a ruin. On the hillside above he placed the folly known as the Eyecatcher, a double-arched flint structure, clearly visible from the house and its terrace walk; it was the first of its kind. A contemporary said that 'the garden is Daphne in little; the sweetest little groves, streams, glades, porticoes, cascades and river imaginable; all the scenes are perfectly classic'. So much admired was Kent's layout that a separate gate through which visitors might enter was erected by the side of the main road. Where Kent led, others followed, and the ultimate in follies was created with the remodelling in the 1790s of Strattenborough Castle Farm near Coleshill to resemble a ruined battlemented dwelling.

Kent was only doing, to perfection, what others were doing elsewhere. A house at Shotover was built, perhaps by William Townesend of Oxford, between 1714 and 1718. The garden can still be visited; its original formal layout contained long avenues and cross walks, with a canal and a temple to catch the eye. Kent added to it a domed octagonal temple and an obelisk, linked by serpentine walks. Gardens were all the rage. At Wroxton, home of the politically powerful North family, the squire of Radway, Sanderson Miller, in need of money, was one of several to participate in landscaping the grounds. He constructed a lake and a Grand Cascade viewed from a domed temple and overlooked by an obelisk and from a sham battlemented archway still further away. He added the chapel to the house which, seen as old-fashioned, called forth scorn from several visitors. One at least commended the garden, observing that 'the scene consists of a beautiful lake entirely shut in with wood; the head falls into a fine cascade, and that into a serpentine river, over which is a little Gothic seat like a round temple, lifted up by a shaggy mount'. No comment was made on the dovecote which still stands on a bluff by the entrance front.

Activities on a scale similar to that of Nuneham Courtenay took place at Pusey where in 1746 its owner obtained licence to close an old road, adding the land to his park and remodelling the house, the church and much of the village, which was moved out of sight. At Middleton Stoney although the house was rebuilt in the 1750s, described as little better than a hunting lodge, it was only later that Lord Jersey enlarged his park so that it absorbed the village. Finally, in the 1820s, the houses were moved to border the newly-aligned Oxford to Brackley turnpike. Constructed under the watchful eye of Lady Jersey, a contemporary remarked that the new cottages, with their rustic porches and flower gardens, gave an idea of the comfort and respectability seldom enjoyed by the lower classes.

Interest in church building was not always spurred on by a landowner's desire to resite an entire village. Churches built anew were erected in the style already old, and owing a great deal to Sir Christopher Wren's rebuilding of the City churches lost in the Great Fire of 1666. The square ground plan solved the problem posed by the continued presence of the medieval chancel which post-Reformation liturgical practice rendered obsolete; flat ceilings, rather than open timbers, increased the audibility of the sermon, the central point of eighteenth and nineteenth-century services. Sermons also necessitated the design of impressive pulpits and the provision of seating, preferably draughtproof; the box pews typical of the eighteenth century are to be seen, for example, at Chiselhampton, built in 1762. These pews were rented out by the churchwardens, who priced and allocated them by social rank. The lower classes might be relegated to the galleries, as were the choir and musicians, or they might be left to stand. This system came to an end in the mid-nineteenth century when the Church Commissioners, brought into existence in 1818, often replaced the box pews, which provided very little seating proportionate to the floor space they required, with the bench pews familiar today; the seating was made free. Record of their activities, painted on boards displayed in the porch, often remains, for example at Letcombe Bassett.

There was also a revival of interest in church decoration. At Weston on the Green the builders took into the church the ideas underlying the decoration of a country house, providing a plaster ceiling and plaster pilaster doorways; at Kingston Bagpuize a classical temple was constructed. Banbury dynamited its medieval church before rebuilding in contemporary fashion in classically inspired style. At Wallingford St Peter's, where the nave and tower had been redesigned in the 1760s, a spire was added in 1777 which aroused controversy as bitter as any sparked off today by shopping malls.

Funerary monuments were much affected by the opposing ideas of Classical urn and the glory of Man. A bank of monuments at Spelsbury commemorates the Lee family of Ditchley; Sir Edward Turner of Ambrosden erected a massive classical urn to himself and his two wives at Bicester; at Steeple Aston Judge Page, in full legal robes and periwig, reclines on one elbow above his dumpy wife, shown *en deshabille* and propped on bolsters. If, however, the adornment of the church might be impressive, the building itself and the living conditions of the clergy rarely matched it. Many parishes were served by non-resident clergy, some of them fellows of Oxford colleges near enough not to need accommodation; others were too poor to support a priest, others had no congregation. The rector of Heythrop in 1738 refused even to attempt morning services because 'to be sent on a Sunday morning to Heythrop to read to the church walls ... is to me a melancholy consideration'.

The passion and the bitterness between Anglican and Dissenters had passed. The vicar of Bladon in 1738 remarked on 'that general decline of zeal and inclination to divine things in any shape, by which most men are now-a-days become but too indifferent to religion in every shape. Hence also there are, in all places, more absentees than dissenters'. The nonconformist element, however, received impetus from the preaching of a young Oxford graduate, John Wesley. He preached his first sermon at South Leigh in 1725 and was active, especially in the western part of the county, from then until the 1770s; he visited Burford and Witney frequently, commenting on the latter's inhabitants that 'this is such a people as I have not seen: so remarkably diligent in business, and at the same time of so quiet a spirit, and so calm and civil in behaviour'. During the eighteenth century some of the earliest nonconformist chapels were built, notably at Cote by Bampton and at Aston Tirrold for the Baptists, and at Charlbury and Adderbury for the Society of Friends.

Their congregations now contained some men of substance, for it was not only the landed aristocracy who prospered. The smaller tradesmen were also doing well, people like the Strongs of Taynton and the Earlys at Witney. Here this Quaker family was influential in obtaining a charter in 1711 to regulate the blanket weaving industry, which permitted it to function along the lines of a medieval guild, establishing and checking on weight, quality and prices, disciplining members and supervising entry and apprenticeships. They established headquarters in the Blanket Hall, built for them in 1720 at a cost of £430. It had a hall, a Great Room, and an Assistants Room well furnished with 'a dozen and a half of chairs', a chest with two locks and two keys in which were kept 'all the books, writings and evidences' and all ready moneys and securities for moneys. A further £21 3s.4d. was paid the next year for a public striking clock with a bell in a tower on the roof. The clock face and its single hand was added later. A second family which rose during the eighteenth century was the Baptist Bliss family of Chipping Norton, another story in which the apprentice married the master's daughter and, his wedding present a mill, was established in business.

These manufactured goods required outlets for sale beyond local demand, a slowly increasing population wanted luxury goods, factories and families alike needed fuel, for the region, once heavily wooded, was now short of timber. The next wave of expansion, concerned with travel, encouraged the growth of a class of engineers, surveyors and contractors.

Some of the most far-reaching changes of the century came with the turn-piking of the roads. The Tudor statutes, requiring householders in every parish to give six days unpaid labour to the maintenance of roads, had long been inadequate to cope with an ever-increasing volume of long distance traffic. The Turnpike Acts authorised justices of the peace and turnpike trustees to improve stretches of road, collecting tolls from goods and pas-senger vehicles to do so at points where a counterbalanced pole turned hor-izontally on a pivot – the turnpike. A series of private Acts resulted in a series of public roads, not, of course, laid out from pure generosity, but in the belief that they would benefit both trade and the investors' pockets. The aims are clearly set out in the preamble to the Act of 1752 concerning the Wallingford to Faringdon turnpike when the gentlemen, clergy and free-holders of the Vale of the White Horse petitioned

> the same is an exceedingly rich and fertile Vale, of great extent, both as to length and breadth, and producing annually quantities of corn, butter and cheese, which for want of good roads and markets, are rendered almost useless to the publick, and that the farms are hereby impoverished, and farmers very frequent-ly ruined: but that the petitioners apprehend that in case a good road be made through the Vale, and an easy communication opened to the river of Thames, and Cities of London and Westminster, it must necessarily be productive of good effects, not only to the Vale of Berkshire but to many other parts of the kingdom.

Despite the hoped-for advantages progress was erratic and slow, even though some of the new turnpikes were old established routes. The first to become a turnpike was the London-Stokenchurch-Oxford-Woodstock road in 1718; the connection from Woodstock to Chipping Norton and on to Stratford was laid out in 1730. In 1736 the alternative London-Oxford route via Henley and Dorchester was turnpiked, and the route from Oxford via Hanborough to Witney, Burford and Northleach in 1751. A road north to Banbury was laid out in 1756. This joined the Banbury to Buckingham road (1744) at Twyford and connected at Banbury to roads radiating northwards to Warwick (1744), Coventry (1754) and Daventry (1765). In 1756-57 the Oxford to Brackley road was piked.

Many of the roads across the county were not made turnpikes until the 1770s or even later. There was much activity centred on Chipping Norton in the 1770s; the Burford-Chipping Norton-Banbury road and the Chipping Norton-Deddington-Buckingham route in 1770 were followed in 1793 by the road from Chipping Norton through Enstone and Lower Heyford to Bicester. Burford's southward connections were extended to Faringdon and, via Bampton and Tadpole Bridge, to Buckland in 1771 and to Lechlade in 1792. Faringdon's connections across the Vale to Wantage were established in 1752, and to Oxford in 1768. The cross road from Wallingford to Thame was piked in 1768.

In some cases the route was entirely new. Beyond Woodstock, the medieval route, through Wootton, Glympton, Radford, Clevely and Neat Enstone, was abandoned. In an effort at least as dislocating as the construction of any modern road, a new road was laid out on the other side of the Glyme valley, the present A44, 'commenced by ploughing up the whole length of it, and the furrow thus ploughed was six miles in length, the team ploughing the whole length from end to end'. The turnpike to Banbury regularised the direct connection from Oxford, replacing the old route through Woodstock to Rousham Gap. In other instances the already established road was found to require major realignment. In particular, the line over Shotover Hill into Oxford, still to be followed in the Country Park, was abandoned and the road, the modern A40, adjusted to its present course in the 1770s. Rather later, in 1812, the road at Burford, was realigned to avoid the steep descent into the town. The making of the 'top road' and the building of a coaching inn, now the Cotswold Gateway, at the top of the hill, initiated the town's decline. In its turn this alignment has been superseded by the new A40 cut in 1990. The new roads also made some of the older routes redundant; for example the improvement of the Botley causeway in conjunction with a new turnpike westwards out of Oxford in the 1770s made the turnpike preferable to the line over Wytham hill. It meant too that traffic from Witney no longer had to go round via Bladon and Yarnton to approach Oxford from the north, but could take the shorter route over the Thames.

New roads required new river crossings; some of the older bridges were strengthened, others were built to carry the heavier traffic expected on the new roads, for example Tadpole and Swinford bridges, the latter replacing a ferry and part of a scheme to generate money for the debt-laden earls of Abingdon. The toll, of one penny per wheel, is still levied, though it failed to rescue the failing Abingdon family fortunes.

Although the potential for mobility was increased, it did not follow that travel was achieved more quickly or more comfortably. The agricultural scientist, Arthur Young, made his earliest journeys through the county in the 1760s over roads 'in a condition formidable to the bones of all who travelled on wheels'. In 1809, fifty years later, he admitted that a 'noble change' had overtaken the roads and the turnpikes he thought 'very good and, where gravel was obtainable excellent, while even the parish roads were greatly improved'.

The county's towns through which travellers passed were not large places. Many, however, had acquired the three-storey facades best seen now at Wallingford, Watlington, Thame and Faringdon, but once typical of every town. Travellers might refresh themselves at inns while the coach horses were changed; some fine examples of coaching inns, with a wide archway leading into the yard and stables, are to be seen at Henley, Benson, Enstone, Bicester and Dorchester. Toll houses were another essential; their distinctive bay fronts allowed the keeper a clear view of the road, while their back quarters are an interesting sidelight on the accommodation thought necessary for the working class. Two examples remain in Oxford itself; on the Banbury road just north of the bypass and on the Botley Road beyond the railway bridge. Others are at Stadhampton, Dorchester, Charlbury and on the A420 at Longworth. At Swinford bridge the boards displaying the charges are still a reference point. Milestones too had to be erected; most of those in Oxfordshire were either removed or defaced at the beginning of the Second War, whereas those in the Vale are still to be traced along the edges of many of the old turnpikes.

The construction of bridges, often with very long 'lead-in' causeways focused attention on the unreliable nature of the Thames and also made the waterway less attractive to boat traffic. Some bridges were built with special provision for barges, having arches much wider and higher, for example at Radcot bridge and at Sutton Courtenay. At both, a new cut was made specially for barge traffic. A series of very bad floods in the late 1760s gave new life to Yarranton's idea of controllable waterways. Thoughts turned to the feasibility of constructing a canal northwards from Oxford as far as Coventry. Early in 1768 the plan was accepted. Fifty thousand pounds was subscribed immediately, and the town clerks of Coventry, Banbury and Oxford prepared a Bill that received the royal assent in April 1769.

Engineered by the experienced James Brindley, the canal reached Banbury in 1775, but the extension south to Oxford was not completed until 1790, delayed by an inadequate supply of water and by inadequate finance. The resultant fall in prices of many essential commodities encouraged the cutting of a second canal, the Wiltshire and Berkshire, begun in 1795. It started from Abingdon, where its outfall into the Thames is still to be seen, and ended at Semington near Trowbridge where there was a connection into the Kennet and Avon canal, making a total length of fifty-one miles. Two branches allowed access to Wantage and to Longcot near Shrivenham. The canal remained open until 1914; traces of it remain in Wantage and some stretches are still clear on the ground, for example north of Kingston Lisle. The Oxford Canal basin was sold in 1936; round it rise the buildings of Nuffield College. The rest of the canal is still open, functioning as a pleasure waterway. Locks at Claydon, wharves at Banbury and Enslow, a canal village with its own pub, the Rock of Gibraltar, together with some fine brick bridges, are its contribution to the landscape.

The immediate benefit was to enable the easier and infinitely cheaper transport of coal to an area where the only fuel, wood, had long been both costly and scarce. Several towns benefited immediately with the arrival of cheap Warwickshire coal, Banbury, Chipping Norton, Witney and Wantage in particular. Ironworks were established almost immediately at Banbury and Oxford where one factory, now Lucy's, is still in business. The Bliss mill at Chipping Norton began to use steam-powered engines. Witney's mills also changed over to steam power provided by cheaper coal hauled from a depot at Eynsham, supplied via the Thames. The mills used the same route in reverse for transport of their manufactured goods.

The region benefited from the new road system. After the improvement of the London road via Stokenchurch and the construction of a new spur with an easier descent into Oxford from the point where the road turned north towards Islip and Bletchingdon more and more traffic poured into the town. Around 1770 approximately two hundred coaches a day had to negotiate the main streets in which the markets were still held. The Oxford Mileways Act of 1771 was primarily concerned with making the city's streets 'more safe and commodious for traffic'. The old gates were demolished, the streets widened and a market hall built, with the aim of ridding the main streets of 'untidy, messy and unsavoury stalls'. The new building, 'on an extensive scale' and still in use, was thought by contemporaries to be the best of its kind in England. It was described in a guidebook of 1791.

> At the south entrance from the High-street it contains forty commodious shops for butchers. North of these are eight others equally commodious, occupied by gardeners etc., between which are two spacious collonades for poultry, eggs, bacon, cheese, etc. divided into forty stalls; and beyond these extending quite to Jesus College Lane, is a large area for country gardeners, fruit and divers other commodities.

There were other improvements. At the city limits to the north the Radcliffe Infirmary opened with thirty-six beds in 1770. To the west, the castle gaol was rebuilt, finished by its keeper, Daniel Harris; he contrived that 'the great part of the work should be done by convicts, several of whom by their industry and manifest reformation have obtained their release'. Its plan was very similar to the gaol at Abingdon he executed in 1805.

Many of these changes, especially in the countryside, are perhaps best understood by looking at the maps of the Vale by John Rocque, made in 1761, and of Oxfordshire by Richard Davis in 1794. Separated by only thirty years Rocque recorded a landscape very close to that of the middle ages; he shows the unenclosed fields, the line of most of the roads before the establishment of the turnpike trusts or the cutting of the canal. Davis, on the other hand, reveals a landscape in transition; the earliest parliamentary enclosures are shown, albeit schematically and many of the turnpike roads familiar to us today. Both maps also show mills, the majority still water-driven, but some the newer windmills, one of which still stands at Wheatley.

Thanks to only mild participation in the factors making wealthy magnates to the north, Oxfordshire became a haven for those same tycoons, such as the Birmingham industrialist Matthew Robinson Boulton who bought Great Tew in 1815. The county was sheltered from the Industrial Revolution by its geography. It had no outlet to the sea, and no recognised natural resources other than water power despite Dr Plot's dark hints, recently substantiated, of a coalfield underlying central Oxfordshire. Its inhabitants continued to enjoy agricultural fortunes, and it was here that the biggest changes took place. Experiment with new methods of farming made it clear that the scattered ownership of small strips of the medieval open field system did not lend themselves to efficient management or more intensive exploitation.

The result was the enclosing of common land and the division of the open fields, in which a number of owners held strips of land, into the tidy parcels of land hedged about, thought of as the typical English landscape. The effect of assessing the extent of land held as scattered strips and reallocating the agreed acreage as neat blocks of land was to enrich the wealthy and impoverish the less well off, who had supplemented their wages by growing extra food, grazing cattle, cutting turves for fuel or gathering firewood on the common land.

The enclosure movement was no new process. The effects of the Black Death and the Tudor preference for ownership of complete parish had already forced enclosure, for example at Brookend and Bletchingdon. But these were scattered instances, accounting for only 13% of total agricultural land by 1730. The widespread change came in the 1770s and 1780s; thirty-three acts affected the region in the 1770s, thirty-five in the next decade; even so only about half the county was enclosed by 1810. A second wave followed in the decades after the Napoleonic wars; the process went on, with decreasing urgency through the nineteenth century. It began on the rich Redlands of the north and at much the same time in the Vale, both areas where villages had retained the medieval two-field system longest and where owners therefore reaped the greatest benefits by bringing more land under permanent cultivation. It spread last to the wooded areas of the Chilterns and to Wychwood.

Enclosure was not a cheap process and was one in which only the wealthy could participate. Money was needed first for legal fees to draft the private bill requiring parliamentary consent which the major landowners of the parish had to obtain to acquire the legal right to enclose common land. After this, the Commissioners sent to assess and apportion the land had to be paid. When that had been achieved, the new plots still had to be separated by fences. The letters of one enclosing owner give us a glimpse of the whole process. John Sibthorp, Professor of Botany at Oxford University, bought the estate of South Leigh for about £8000 in 1782. He considered that he had made a good purchase which would bring in a return of 3½%. Nevertheless, he admitted that although he saw his property 'greatly improving' it would be through the medium of large expenditure. The Act and the Commissioners who surveyed the land cost him £2000. He still had to fence and gate the new plots, which he did largely with the timber from two to three thousand trees cut down on the estate. He seems to have lost most of his woodland, though sentiment dictated that he would 'reserve one tree here and there which stands single in a field to surround with a rural bench'.

He employed fifty-four men as carpenters, masons, hedgers, ditchers, roadmen and woodmen, for fencing was only a part of many changes. Roads were laid out to give access from the village centre to new fields and new farmhouses. Although some utilised existing tracks, others appear to have been laid out with a ruler; their width was usually fixed at not less than forty feet, more often sixty feet from hedge to hedge, so that in muddy conditions carriages, carts and coaches still had space in which to dodge the worst of the ruts and potholes. The existence of these roads is betrayed still where a narrow macadam strip runs between broad grass verges bordered by thick hedges. Improbable as it seems, Five Mile Drive in north Oxford has its origins as such a road, the short cut between the Woodstock and the Banbury roads.

The other major change was the building of farmhouses and outbuildings on new sites, for it became more convenient for the owner to live at the centre of his newly rearranged fields than to return every night to the village. Many isolated farmsteads date from this period, some recognisable as typical buildings of the late eighteenth century, often by the side of a new road for example at Nether Worton and Alkerton Fields. Some nineteenth-century square farmhouses are also a delayed result of enclosure; the owner lived in his old house in the village until it decayed beyond mending; abandoning it, he built himself a fine new residence, apparently in the middle of nowhere. Many of the older village farms were given to the labourers for their accommodation, divided into smaller dwellings.

The effect on agriculture was beneficial; in 1809 Arthur Young maintained that during the previous twenty years 'the husbandry has considerably improved in every particular; if you go into Banbury market next Thursday you may distinguish the farmers from inclosures from those in open fields – quite a different sort of men – the farmers as much changed as their husbandry, quite new men in point of knowledge and ideas'.

Like the costs, the benefits belonged to the wealthy. Though it was a subject for debate by contemporaries, for the less well-off enclosure generally meant a drop in living standards because of the loss of rights in the common land – of far greater importance than legal rights in land they did not even have. Some contemporaries argued that enclosure provided work; some, indeed, of the new crops and new agricultural techniques did generate new jobs and new crafts. Nevertheless many observed that poverty was increasing. It was correctly attributed to rising prices with wages lagging behind. Other causes were loss of jobs for women and children in the increasingly mechanised weaving industry. An increase in population did not help.

The effect of the changes overall on the parish of Deddington were described in 1797.

> The high rates in this parish are ascribed to the common-field, of which the land principally consists; whereas the neighbouring parishes have been inclosed many years, and many small farms in them have been consolidated; so that many small farmers with little capitals, have been obliged, either to turn labourers, or to procure small farms in Deddington, or other parishes, that possess common field. Besides this, the neighbouring parishes are, many of them, possessed by a few individuals, who are cautious in permitting newcomers to obtain a settlement.

> The general opinion here is, that canals are a great injury to the poor, by enabling farmers to send their corn abroad ... A boat laden with flour was lately seized by the populace, but was restored, on the miller's promising to sell it at a reduced price.

> This parish contains, by estimation, 4000 acres. The number of houses that pay the window-tax is 102; the number exempted near 300. The inhabitants ... are mostly employed in agriculture. There are ten inns, or ale-houses in the parish; the number, a few years ago, was 21. The principal articles of cultivation are wheat, barley and beans. There are about 45 acres of common in the parish.

By the 1830s the social consequences of the long drawn-out wars with France and of the increasing use of machinery in both factories and farms were becoming noticeable. Soldiers and sailors returned to discover there were no jobs and their families were without means of support other than help from the parish rates. Little wonder that in 1830 riots broke out, at their worst round Wantage where forty-seven prisoners were tried. One was transported and thirty-five imprisoned, though the only death sentence was commuted to eighteen months' imprisonment. The enclosure of marshy Otmoor near Oxford, finally achieved in 1831, also had the immediate effect of increasing distress there. The newly drained land was reduced in value, contrary to all expectations. Too many people lost the fringe benefits they had had from fishing and fowling. Out of a population of 1700, only seventy-three received any land and, of these, more than half received less than ten acres. Hedging, ditching and draining operations were expensive, so that only the larger and richer landowners could afford to pay for them. Floods resulting from the new channel cut for the river Ray, which damaged land previously dry, proved to be the last straw. Twenty-nine farmers united to cut the dykes to allow the river to return to its old course. They were sued, indicted for felony and acquitted by the courts. The verdict encouraged others and wholesale uprooting of fences began. A contemporary described how

> the depredators increased in number greatly, and came in disguise with their faces blackened, and some with partly women's clothes; they began cutting down some trees of about ten years' growth...whenever a tree fell, a shout of exultation was raised with a blowing of horns, heard at a distance of about 2-3 miles. The assemblage had begun between eight and nine o'clock and continued their ravages of pulling up posts and rails, cutting the live quickset hedges and trees until about twelve when they retired; the watch was completely paralysed by the opposed numbers

The Oxfordshire Militia was summoned and was confronted by a mass perambulation of about one thousand men, women and children. The Riot Act was read and later some sixty-six men arrested, forty-one of them being sent by waggon to Oxford. The sequel is best told in the words of *Jackson's Oxford Journal* :

> At some distance from this city, the detachment were met by the mob, which continually increased, and which attacked them with stones, bricks, sticks etc., calling out to the prisoners to make their escape. The fair at St Giles ... had assembled vast numbers of the worst description of people, and in passing through the streets the yeomanry were assailed with the utmost violence, and

Above: Aston Tirrold chapel

Left: Chiselhampton Church

Below left: Watlington, Crouching Street

Below: Oxford Canal at Claydon

Above: The Bliss Mill, Chipping Norton

Left: Abingdon Gaol

Below right: Elms Parade, Botley, Oxford

Below left: Henley fountain

many of them seriously injured... The rioters had latterly increased to the number of several thousands, and it became utterly impossible for the small party of the military to prevent the prisoners, consisting of double their number, and who were unbound, from making their way out of the waggons, assisted as they were by the mob.

Later, a subscription for their aid was opened by an Oxford wine merchant; in practical terms the matter had come to an end.

Victorian and Edwardian Times 1832-1914

The discontent which had come to a head at Wantage, Bicester and Otmoor was part of the nation-wide unrest which preceded the reforming decade of the 1830s and was the background to the enactment of the parliamentary Reform Bill of 1832. The newly enfranchised members of the House of Commons enacted new measures; some at least were aimed at the improvement of life at the lower end of the social scale, a foretaste of the growing body of legislation which would affect the county throughout the century.

There were other, physical, changes, their effects still visible today. The draining of Otmoor, the taming of the river Thames flooding and the clearing of Wychwood forest altered the appearance of the countryside. That of the towns was affected by successive waves of legislation which created the need for municipal buildings and by the increase of population which demanded new housing. The advent of the railways affected marketing patterns and changed both leisure and working habits by increasing the opportunities for mobility. Lastly the city of Oxford began to expand far beyond its medieval bounds.

Floods were no new phenomenon in the Thames valley where the river regularly overflowed its banks. In 1821 the surveyor for the Thames Commissioners reported that the river 'would be running in its natural course' were it not for the large number of man-made weirs, intended to facilitate navigation, fishing or mills, which constricted its width. Improved drainage of fields, usually resulting from their enclosure and the owner's desire to increase his yields, also meant that more water found its way to the river. The problem got worse after the 1840s when cheap machine-made drainage pipes became readily available.

The river was already suffering as a means of transport from competition from the turnpikes and the canals, and more recently from the newly laid out railways. Schemes of improvement were regularly formulated and as regularly defeated by the river users. Even the Thames Conservancy, formed in 1866, was no more successful in improving conditions until three consecutive years' flooding occurred in 1875-77. When in this latter year flood waters left Queen Victoria high, but at least dry, in Windsor Castle, action was finally taken. A further inquiry, and further floods in 1882-83, brought about the Thames Preservation Act of 1885 which for the first time mentioned another use 'the purposes of public recreation' and 'regulating the pleasure traffic'. Only in the 1890s did the Commission have sufficient finance and adequate powers to start building pound locks and weirs on the Upper Thames. Their efforts included also the straightening of the river's meanders; the cut at Shifford left the ancient ford at Duxford without importance except as a passage for agricultural machinery and animals over a sluggish backwater.

The days of water transport were virtually finished and the redevelopment of the river as a source of pleasure was already under way. The Regatta at Henley was instituted in 1839; the moorings filled up with intricately carved and decorated barges for onlookers and rowing teams alike. Another stretch of the river below Folly Bridge at Oxford was utilised for college races. For the lower classes Salter's offered steamer excursions and picnics, for example on Picnic Island belonging to Lord Harcourt of Nuneham Courtenay where, by arrangement with the estate steward, groups could hold parties and light bonfires. The same desire to escape urban life emerges in the pages of *Three Men in a Boat*, which, published in 1889, recounted the adventures of three bored bachelors taking to the 'rough life' and rowing themselves up the Thames from Kingston upon Thames to Oxford.

The book was a fair comment on the status of the waterway following the advantages brought by the coming of the railways. They increased personal mobility, made the transport of goods cheaper, thus stimulating industry and indirectly affecting the growth of towns. Entirely a matter of private enterprise, lines wound across the countryside, some instantly profitable, some the result of local vested interests, others ill-conceived speculative ventures.

The Great Western Railway's main line from London to Bristol cut across the Vale in 1840-41; a branch line from Didcot to Oxford was finally constructed, after much opposition from the University, in 1844. Within seven years Oxford had links to Bicester and Bletchley, to Banbury and, by 1853, through the Evenlode valley to Charlbury, Kingham and Worcester. Kingham became the junction for a line opened to Chipping Norton in 1855, to help the Bliss mills, and extended twenty years later through Hook Norton, Bloxham and Adderbury to Banbury to facilitate the transport of iron ore. By that time another company's line connected Oxford to Witney and Fairford (1861), opening up the southwest of the area, while another linked Oxford, Thame and Aylesbury by 1864, doing the same for the southeast. Watlington was linked to Princes Risborough in 1872. Branch lines from the Great Western's routes provided services to Abingdon,

Wallingford, Wantage and Faringdon. A line from Didcot to Newbury and Southampton started operation in 1882. Bicester's direct connection to London came only in 1905, Banbury's in 1910. Only Burford was overlooked by the network.

Like the turnpikes, the impact of the railways on the landscape was considerable. Although there are only two striking viaducts, those at Somerton, and two tunnels, at Chipping Norton and Horspath, embankments and bridges were frequently needed and, in use or neglected, are visible still. Isambard Kingdom Brunel built a bridge over the Thames near Moulsford and designed several stations, one of which is still used at Culham, of 'Tudor Gothic' brick. Banbury, Bicester and Oxford, served by more than one company, had two stations each; Oxford's second, adjacent to its former rival, is at present heavily disguised as a used car tyre depot. Land in town centres had to be set aside for sheds and sidings; now out of commission it is used at Oxford for a Fire Station and in Banbury for housing.

The impact on peoples' lives was just as forceful. Cheaper transport of goods opened new markets, cheap travel new horizons for many who had never before ventured further than the local market town. Day trips to a wide variety of destinations were available; from Witney, for example, there was a choice of Bala, Brighton, Weymouth, Liverpool, Torquay, Hastings, Southampton, Blackpool and Weston-super-Mare.

Some places acquired importance from the railway they had not had before. At Kingham, a station hotel, now a nursing home, graced the junction of the Oxford, Worcester & Wolverhampton line with the Bourton on the Water and Chipping Norton branch lines. Steventon functioned briefly as the place where the meetings of the directors of the Great Western Railway were held, since it lay halfway between London and Bristol. A hotel, now converted into private housing, was built close to the station for the purpose until, soon afterwards, Didcot became the Great Western's railway headquarters. Kidlington began its career as a commuter town, foreshadowing the great developments in the south of the county where the railway first made possible the speedy transport of market garden produce to London's ever-hungry markets – watercress from Letcombe Bassett, cheese from Buscot, apples and pears from the Didcot region. Rather later, the commuter links to London from Henley made it possible for many more people to live in the country and travel to work in Town. Thus both Henley and Goring increased in size, their river fronts fringed with large villas set in extensive gardens, their hinterland studded with larger houses set in parks, while the narrow streets of the town centres were packed close with small brick-built terrace houses for the shopkeepers and craftsmen who supplied daily needs. Even places like Cholsey, the junction for Wallingford, could boast some astonishing buildings erected at the end of the century, though none rivalled the Gothic brickwork of Friar's Court, Henley. The railway also had dramatic effects on the Bicester area which saw the construction of hunting lodges easily accessible from the capital.

Further north, the long-established industrial centres received a boost from the widening ease of communications to markets further afield. Witney and Chipping Norton benefited from coal made still cheaper because of rail transport, giving a much needed impetus to the mills. Banbury, the meeting place of three modes of transport, canal, road and rail, was opened up to the north and the midlands as well as to the south. Several firms manufacturing agricultural machinery were set up in the town; Gardner's in 1818, later bought by the German-born Samuelson whose Britannia Works came to dominate the town's life, and overshadow his two competitors, Lampitt's Vulcan Factory and Barrow's Churchill Works. By the end of the century Banbury had overtaken Abingdon as the second town in the area.

Changes in towns, however, came as much from legislation as from industrial growth. The Poor Law of 1834, which banded parishes into groups for administrative convenience in dealing with the poor, demanded the building of workhouses. Those at Thame and Chipping Norton survive, the latter used as housing, the former now Rycotewood College. The style was distinctive and their plans similar; a central block for dining, recreation and laundry, separate wings for sleeping accommodation for men, women and children. The establishment of the police force in the 1840s required the building of police stations with offices and cells. Examples are to be seen at Abingdon and Chipping Norton; they made the old lock-ups, for example at Wheatley and Stonesfield, redundant.

Educational measures too have left their mark, though it was not until the Education Act of 1870 that the State set up School Boards to erect buildings; before then the nonconformist British School Society and the Anglican National School Society each made provision for its own. Only one public school was established, Radley College. Libraries were commonly the result of private generosity. Banbury's free library was given to the town by Bernhard Samuelson in 1884, Bicester's by Lord Jersey in 1872, Wallingford's in 1871 and Abingdon's in 1894.

Still prominent in every town centre are the Victorian town halls, replacements of older buildings no longer adequate: Bampton (1838), Chipping Norton (1842), Banbury's second in 1854, Thame (1888) and Henley (1900). Only the care of the sick and the elderly remained firmly in private hands, sometimes in the cottage hospitals, sometimes in almshouses, many of which were rebuilt.

Some of a town's other finest buildings, emphasising the still agricultural basis of the county's wealth, were the result of increasing specialisation. Corn Exchanges, the places where crops were bought and sold, were built at Wallingford, Witney, Faringdon, Wantage and Abingdon; two were erected at Banbury, the consequence of trade rivalries. Markets themselves, however, were removed from town centres to their fringes, near the railway station where possible. Increasingly, shops were taking over the centre, while annual fairs and weekly markets declined, sometimes, as at Deddington, Bampton and Burford, to extinction.

As the century went on more and more attention was paid to measures which would prevent, or at least limit, the spread of disease. Water companies were formed at Banbury in 1856, at Chipping Norton in 1878 and at Henley in 1880. Sewerage schemes followed quickly. Smaller places, including even Bicester and Deddington, remained dependent on springs and wells till the end of the century, while in many villages of west Oxfordshire the fountain became a central feature, for example at Charlbury, Churchill, Taston, Spelsbury, Over Norton, Church Enstone, Hethe, Henley and Wallingford. The most splendid example is the Maharajah's Well at Stoke Row where a cast iron cupola rises high over the well shaft, some 368 feet deep. Its construction, and its keeper, were paid for by the Maharajah of Benares, appalled to think his friend the Governor should suffer problems with his water supply on retiring to England in 1864!

Although the increase in the size of the region's towns was insignificant compared to the growth taking place in the northern industrial areas, Abingdon, Banbury, Chipping Norton, Bicester, Faringdon, Wantage and Witney all increased, although Burford, Islip, Eynsham, Bampton and Charlbury declined. Oxford, of course, was always the largest, not because of any industry that flourished there, but because of the University. Its population increased by nearly 300% between 1801 and 1901, but it is one of the many paradoxes in the history of the city that it began to expand at a time when it seemed to be at its most lifeless.

Till the opening of the GWR Oxford enjoyed considerable advantages from being on the great roads leading northward to Birmingham and Shrewsbury and westward to Cheltenham, Gloucester and South Wales. Between twenty and thirty coaches used daily to pass through the town, and its inns were the largest in England; but this source of wealth is now almost extinct, and owing to the opposition of the University the railway was, for many years, kept at a distance from the city. There are no manufactures; and the trade of the place is chiefly confined to the supply of the academic inhabitants.

The richer tradesmen were responsible for the earliest development of the suburb of North Oxford, including Park Town begun in 1854. The area was later developed by St John's College and subsequently taken over by university families after 1877 when dons were permitted to marry. The huge residences, adorned with ridiculously extravagant pseudo-Gothic ornamentation, were a far cry from the humble houses of Jericho round the University Press, the close-packed alleys of St Ebbe's or of Hayfield Road, a street of terrace houses built by the Oxford Industrial and Provident Building Society in 1886-88.

The expansion of housing in Oxford is paralleled in the smaller towns, partly because of a natural increase in population and partly because of a steady drift to urban centres. However, it was never the role of the State, and only rarely of the employer, to provide houses for the work force. The need had to be filled by the speculative builder, who bought the land, divided it into plots and sold the houses he built, sometimes to his own design, sometimes from pattern books and sometimes to a client's specifications. The two-storey brick terrace is familiar in every town in the region. At Banbury a new suburb grew up, New Grimsbury, while a bricklayer turned builder, William Wilkins, erected thirty-seven houses along The Causeway between 1856 and 1871. These were houses built to minimum specifications. Others, elsewhere, were more substantial, for at example in King's, Clarence and York Roads in Henley and in Newbury Street, Wantage. Some of the more unusual were built for the middle classes, for example the planned suburb of Albert Park in Abingdon, where a series of large detached villas were built around Park Crescent, with a statue of Prince Albert the focal point.

Nevertheless, some employers did look after their workforce. Naldertown in Wantage was built around 1870 to house twelve families working at the Nalder's iron foundry; in Old Woodstock the Blenheim estate built several semi-detached cottages and a terrace while the Worcester glover's firm built in Oxford Street, Woodstock. Between 1856 and 1873 the owner of the paper mill at Wolvercote created the street of houses running from the mill to the far end of the green. Fifty years after the need first arose before the Great Western Railway at Didcot finally erected housing for the many it employed.

In the countryside there was a similar problem, only a few estate owners seeing, and meeting, the need for adequate accommodation for their labourers, many of whom inhabited cottages like Styles Cottage, Uffington described in a letter of October 1849 :

You approach the doorway through the mud, over some loose stones, which rock under your feet in using them. You have to stoop for admission and cautiously look around ere you fairly trust yourself within. There are but two rooms in the house – one below and the other above. On leaving the bright light without, the room which you enter is so dark that for a time you can with difficulty discern the objects which it contains. Before you is a large but a cheerless fireplace – it is not every poor man that may be said to have a hearth – with a few smouldering embers of a small wood fire, over which hangs a pot, recently used for some culinary purpose. At one corner stands a small rickety table, whilst scattered about are three old chairs – one without a back – and a stool or two, which, with a very limited and imperfect washing apparatus, and a shelf or two for plates, tea-cups etc. constitute the whole furniture of the apartment. What could be more cheerless or comfortless? And yet you fancy you could put up with everything but the close earthy smell, which you endeavour in vain to escape by breathing very short and quickly.

If this was typical of labourers' living conditions, it explains why Lord Effingham rebuilt the houses at Hardwick soon after his acquisition of the Tusmore estate in 1860 and the necessity for the High Court Order of 1884 compelling the replacement of ruinous cottages by the sturdy two-storey houses which today line the village street at Mixbury. On the estate at West Lockinge action was taken from a feeling of disgust at the 'farm sheds, muck yards and hovels' which crowded the manor house, rather than from any philanthropic motives. Nevertheless, Lady Wantage could truthfully write in the 1890s that

An architect has rarely been employed; plans of buildings have always been made and executed under Lord and Lady Wantage's own superintendence. The picturesque character of the older style of cottage building, with its 'Wattle and daub' walls, rough timber beams and thatched roofs, has been as far as possible retained, with the view of preserving the irregular character and charm of the old Berkshire villages.

Here, however, far more than mere restoration was attempted and most of the houses had three bedrooms, with two living rooms below and a kitchen. There was not, of course, any piped water or internal sanitation, but neither was there in most towns.

A mixture of philanthropy and profiteering lay behind the setting up of Carter's Town, now Carterton. In 1901 William Carter bought land from the Duke of Marlborough and then, trading as Homesteads Ltd, subdivided it and created a colony of smallholders. One purchaser at least was satisfied.

Having just left the army on a pension and being desirous of settling in the coutry I searched in vain to find a comfortable and substantial cottage at a cost within my modest means, until I came across an advertisement of Homesteads Ltd.

I am comfortably settled on one of their estates and have a well built wood and iron bungalow detached, containing six rooms and with a good water supply. This I purchased together with an acre of excellent land for £165, freehold, situated on the main road and two miles from the station. This I think will take some beating.

A different, though not dissimilar, experiment in communal housing had been made earlier by Fergus O'Connor, advocate of a six-point People's Charter aimed at voting rights for all. A secondary development of the original movement aimed to restore to working people their God-given right of access to basic means of survival, the soil. By building houses at affordable prices, O'Connor hoped also to give more people the property qualification necessary to acquire the right to vote. Charterville, established three miles west of Witney in 1848, was the third of five such land settlements. Made up of seventy-eight single-storey three-room cottages, each with its own small holding, and sharing a school and a meeting room, the village was peopled by families who uprooted themselves from urban and industrial areas in order to live off the land. The life was seen as an alternative to commercialism, industrialised capitalism and an answer to the evils of surplus labour, the existence of which kept wages low. Sited on the hilltop above Minster Lovell, bordering the Oxford to Burford turnpike, Charterville was on poor agricultural land, far from water and removed from obvious market outlets; the venture failed. Many of the original settlers had returned home by the early 1850s, leaving local villagers, especially those from Minster Lovell, to buy up and occupy the holdings. None could make a living, but even in the agricultural depression of the 1870s, when many villages became depopulated, Charterville's houses remained occupied. Many can still be seen, as can the larger building intended to be the school.

In that it was planned without either church or chapel Charterville was an oddity. Most new settlements of the nineteenth century were provided with one or the other, often both, for example at Leafield. The new period of church building was made necessary by the creation of new parishes in expanding towns, by the need for structural repairs in existing buildings and by further liturgical changes. Many churches in the county bear the indelible stamp of the indefatigable diocesan architect, G.E.Street. His pupils, William Morris and Philip Webb, both resident at Kelmscott from 1871, propagated their own version of appreciation of earlier values.

Often much larger than necessary for the population of the new parishes they served, new churches were built in Oxford, Henley, Witney, Banbury, Abingdon and Didcot. Many others were enlarged or so heavily restored as to be virtually new, the Victorian restorers being at least as destructive as the iconoclasts of the Reformation. Even more numerous than new Anglican churches were nonconformist churches or chapels. Seven were built between 1800 and 1825; from then until the end of the century another ninety-two were erected, in town and country alike.

Vicarages too, many of them in poor condition, received attention, built bigger and bigger throughout the century. Their increasing size clearly reflects the higher social standing of the clergy. The estimate for the rebuilding of the rectory at Godington in 1787 states that the front of the house was to be thirty-seven feet long. The house was :

> To consist of a parlour with an oak floor, a kitchen, dairy, brew house and pantry, all 8 feet high, with a cellar, an oven to be in the brew house, the dairy to be ceiled and all floored with stone or brick. Three bedrooms each 7 and a half feet high, to be floored with white deal; two garrets to be floored with elm. The house to be tiled and plaistered: Laths to be pinn'd etc.

Such a house, costing £220, was thought to be 'proper and fitting' for a parsonage. Fifty years later, however, so modest a house was considered quite impossible to live in. A contemporary wrote of the vicarage at Charlton on Otmoor that the vicar had rebuilt it 'in a substantial manner, at once calculated to convey to posterity a proof of his superior taste and public spirit'. Almost two thirds of the rectories in the diocese of Oxford were rebuilt between 1800 and 1855. At Great Rollright loans were made to the incumbent in 1783, 1813 and 1822. In 1849 the then vicar pulled the house down to erect a building so large that its upkeep would strain his income. Enormous cellars lay below an airy hall and a wide staircase. During its construction the rector wandered round the site repeatedly demanding 'Give me air .... give me space! Enlarge it here! Enlarge it there!' The cost soared and the rector was unable to leave his house in case he met his creditors. One Sunday morning he announced the text for his sermon: 'Forgive us our debts as we forgive our debtors'. He then disappeared from the pulpit into the vestry and was never seen again.

While building by churchmen might flourish, country house construction was on the wane. The older houses might still be refurbished or remodelled, as were Nuneham Courtenay, Wroxton, Heythrop and Kiddington. At Steeple Barton one of the last parks was laid out to match the rebuilding of the house. Just before the First World War Sibford Ferris' manor house underwent an exuberant make-over in a mixture of architectural styles. Eynsham Hall, Friar's Park at Henley and Shiplake Court are amongst the completely new houses built.

By contrast, there was more building in villages, some of it enforced by population increases, highest between 1840 and 1860. Although it was in the interests of the landowners to restrict house building in case the parish should be swamped by destitute occupiers claiming relief, some villages grew larger. At Lower Heyford houses rose up the hill from the old centre round the bridge; at Steeple Aston South Street developed on the other side of the valley from the church. The straggling houses of Middle Barton came into existence after the road was made a turnpike and men could build on the verges. A similar process had taken place on the county's eastern boundary at Juniper Hill, the model for Larkrise in the book *Larkrise to Candleford*. In 1754 four cottages to house paupers had been built and paid for by the parish of Cottisford. By the 1880s it had grown to

> about thirty cottages and an inn, not built in rows but dotted down anywhere within a more or less circular group. A deeply rutted cart track surrounded the whole, and separate houses or groups of houses were connected by a network of pathways. The church and school were in the mother village, (Cottisford), a mile and a half away.

Villages came into existence as a consequence of the clearance of Wychwood Forest, particularly within the confines of the old forest. At Fordwells, whose spring was one of the forest boundary marks, land was set aside as allotments for the landless men whose labour was needed on the new farms and who had to be housed somewhere. It remains tiny; a scatter of cottages along the roadside, a Primitive Methodist Chapel and a water supply which as late as the 1970s was provided by the springs gushing from the steep valley sides. New Yatt and Mount Skippitt are settlements of similar origin.

Over grazing and under management were the reasons behind the Act for the disafforestation of the ancient royal forest of Wychwood, signed in 1857 in the interest of increasing the land's profitability, and therefore its value, to the Crown. Within two years almost all the trees in its ten square miles had been cut, the timber sold and seven new farmsteads built 'on sites judiciously selected in reference both to the occupation of the land and the beauty of the prospects'. Kingstanding and Chasewood Farms and High Lodge are the three most obviously visible. They were constructed of local stone, the field boundaries and division fences set out, water supplies organised and the land prepared for cultivation. Within two years of the first felling the first tenants were sowing their first crops. What remains now of the Domesday forest lies immediately west of Cornbury Park.

Throughout the century the region remained firmly agricultural. Enclosure continued, enthusiasm peaking from the 1840s to the end of the 1860s and the final two Acts, for Steventon and Crowell, were passed in 1882. At least in the early years of this period developments were taking place which made agriculture more profitable and brought more land under cultivation. One very large change followed the enclosure of the common lands of Bampton in the 1850s when extensive drainage works transformed wet ground into highly productive arable land. Two brooks were widened to act as drainage channels into the Thames; the Great Brook, bordered by a straight road lined with trees, resembles a Dutch rather than an English landscape. There was no rush to build on such land; the only new house, Meadow Farm on the road to Tadpole Bridge, was prudently given three storeys by its builders. When William Morris settled at Kelmscott, he had come to a very empty landscape.

Until the 1870s agricultural fortunes prospered. Thereafter a series of bad seasons and poor harvests, coupled to competition from abroad, resulted in a depression which lasted some thirty-five years. The market in land collapsed, farms could no longer be let, unless at rents reduced by as much as half. The wise landlord took the management of his estate into his own control, thus avoiding renting at uneconomic levels and enjoying economies of scale. Even so, there could be two approaches, the industrial and the paternalistic.

The owner of the Buscot estate decided on full mechanisation. With his purchase of the estate came a short canal, known as Buscot Pill, its wharf, a small brick and tile works, a malt house and a cheese wharf on the river. Squire Campbell, whose fortune came from gold digging in Australia, first constructed two reservoirs to irrigate the estate fields, put under sugar beet. From this Campbell distilled spirit alcohol at the distillery he built on the island next to the lock. To assist delivery of the crop he constructed a narrow gauge railway round the estate and to use up the distillery's waste products he built a mill for the manufacture of oil cake. Another plant produced an artificial fertiliser and vitriol, by-products he could use on his dairy farm which continued the estate tradition of dairy produce for use in London. As an employer Campbell had a good reputation, with a well paid nine hour day for his men and, it was said, a six day week for the cows! But the venture failed and by 1879 the industrial side of the estate had been closed down. All that remains of his buildings is a concrete barn by the present car park.

At Lockinge and Ardington Lord Wantage adopted the more conventional paternalistic approach, though he too kept close control over his lands for which he appointed a manager to replace tenant farmers. In 1893 he detailed some of the advantages:

> In the first place you get a superior sort of agriculturalist to manage the land, a better man in knowledge, both theoretical and practical, in training and in capacity, than the neighbouring farmers, so that he can set an example to the whole county round; farmers see the work better done, and the labourers are not slow to find it out. I employ one head bailiff only for all the land I have in hand (1968 a.). He buys everything and sells everything and under him are only ordinary working foremen. In farming on a large scale there is economy; you can use machinery more advantageously, and you can diminish the number both of labourers and of horses.

Lord Wantage, however, was amongst the more caring landlords, seeing clearly that for many of his tenants, the married men especially, it was hopeless to leave in search of other employment. As well as the improved cottages, Lockinge and Ardington had a cooperative bakery; a nominee managed the pub and ploughed the profits into the village hall and street lighting. Allotments supplemented daily diet, and a small savings scheme was started. Employees' children were assisted, by recommendations, into jobs in trade, the railways or the Services.

Lord Wantage was exceptional. Elsewhere the agricultural labourer was hard hit. If he did not leave for the towns, or emigrate, he signed up, if he dared, with the Union formed first at Milton under Wychwood in April 1872 as an offshoot of the Warwickshire Agricultural Labourers Union or, by the end of 1872, with the branch of the National Union. It aroused the instant opposition of the landowners, scarcely surprising when the local leader wrote to *Jackson's Oxford Journal* that 'there are no cottages in our neighbourhood worse than many of the cottages belonging to the duke of Marlborough'. Lord Wantage, thinking hopes of increasing wages by this means illusory, disapproved, and warned his employees 'against specious promises held out by agitators and by associations'. His attitude killed any local interest, but, in any case, the Union never flourished.

The harshness of an existence which began at dawn and ended at dusk cannot be reconstructed in the County's excellent museums at Cogges and Wantage in which late Victorian life can be studied easily, or at the museum of Bygones at Claydon. The noises too have changed; the clanking thuds of a working steam-powered sawmill can occasionally be heard at the Blenheim estate sawmill at Combe, but the remaining mills at Charney

Basset, the Venn Mill and at Shipton under Wychwood are silent. The Filkins Weavers recreate the conditions of the cottage weaving industry.

By the outbreak of the first World War in August 1914 Oxfordshire was suffering the full impact of the agricultural depression which had begun in the 1870s. The county had slipped from being one of the richest in England to one of the poorest; farm workers' wages were the lowest in the land. Nevertheless, agriculture was still the biggest single employer, possibly a quarter of the whole population being engaged on the land. Efforts to bring in industry had been minimal; cement works opened at Chinnor in 1908, not a large concern. Nor, at the time, was the car factory belonging to William R. Morris, opened in 1912. The city too was stagnant, its largest employer the University, its single largest trade printing.

The Twentieth Century 1914-1996

The immediate effect of the outbreak of war in 1914 was an exodus of the menfolk, from villages, urban centres and the University. A second was the switch to the making of munitions in William Morris's newly opened car factory with a consequent demand for labour; a third was the creation of more new jobs by the establishment of four airfields at Upper Heyford, Witney, Weston on the Green and Bicester, and of an Ordnance Depot at Didcot. The soldiers who survived the fighting returned to find that change resulting from the war continued in earnest. Many men, wounded, were not fit to be employed in heavy agricultural labour. A general shortage of manpower was resolved by increasing mechanisation in farm and factory alike.

Village communities shrank, not just because so many of the male inhabitants had been killed, but because their widows, sweethearts or sisters discovered that in comparison with life in the towns their own living conditions were physically less attractive. One country plumber observed that it was all very well to have a cottage which looked like a Christmas card, but it would be better to have one which was watertight. The now highly prized, highly priced cottages of north Oxfordshire were, in the 1920s and 1930s, damp and draughty, not necessarily watertight under their thatched roofs and rubble walls and might well house man, wife and six or seven children in their two bedrooms. In the inter-war years the rents were so low that landlords could not afford their upkeep, even when they wished to do so. In the late 1930s the general manager of one of the largest building societies observed that

> One cannot move about the countryside without realizing that many of the farmhouses and farm buildings are a social and economic disgrace to Britain. Still more disturbing is the obsolescence, inadequacy of accommodation and the insanitary and derelict condition of a large proportion of the cottages of rural workers.

This situation prevailed despite a series of Housing Acts passed between 1919 and 1942 aimed at the improvement of rural housing by providing finance, either to local councils or to landlords for new building or refurbishment. The new council houses, in a distinctive style, are common sur-

111

vivals; sometimes they are only an isolated pair on the outskirts of a village, sometimes a crescent as at Twyford off the A4260 or at Newland, Witney. While gas, water and electricity were commonplace in urban centres, their provision was far less frequent in the villages, many of which had only pumped, and not mains, water until as late as the 1950s. Part of the problem was practical; too many cottages lay too far off main roads for it to be feasible to connect mains services. Even where supply was available, surprisingly little use was made of electricity except for lighting and even then only in the grander residences or the newly-built council houses. Few private tenants could afford the cost of wiring, few landlords would.

Mechanisation had adverse effects on village trades as the traditional crafts ceased to be needed. Millers, maltsters, coopers, smiths, saddlers and wheelwrights had no place even in areas where 75% of farms were smaller than 150 acres (60.72 ha), making them too small for use of modern equipment. A situation where jobs were few and accommodation was poor could produce only one result; the old might remain, indifferent to change, but the young, dissatisfied, moved to the towns exchanging the often still strongly dependent culture of the village for a sense of freedom, in the shopping arcades and cinemas, in addition to such conveniences as indoor sanitation and weekly, rather than monthly, refuse collections.

By the 1930s machinery was reducing traditional jobs in the countryside, whether in agriculture or in the home-based industries; it was creating jobs in the towns, further accelerating the drift from the villages. Shipton on Cherwell's cement works opened in 1928; exploitation of iron ore had begun at Wroxton in 1920 and Northern Aluminium arrived in Banbury in 1931, replacing the two factories which closed, The Tweed Company and Samuelson's. But the most important were the car factories at Oxford where, by 1926, Morris' works had expanded sufficiently to require the services of two support factories; Pressed Steel was established as a car body manufacturer; Morris took over Osberton Radiators, resiting it in the heart of residential north Oxford.

The effects of his expansion on the city were immediate; between 1921 and 1931 rather more than 13,000 workers were recruited; 43% of them were new to the county. Tentacles of housing spread along the Headington, Cowley and Iffley roads, joining together along the ridge between Rose Hill and Marston. Some was private development, aimed at purchasers, some was funded by the City Council and was intended for rent, for example Weirs Lane at the southern end of the Abingdon Road or the Valentia Road estate, a planned garden suburb on Headington Hill. In one notorious case, at Cutteslowe at the northern end of the Banbury Road, private and council estates adjoined. Oxford City Council began work on an estate of 298 houses, together with two schools, shops and two pubs, the Friar Bacon and the Cherwell Tavern. It sold the remaining land to a private developer with plans to build 208 houses. Though the houses were virtually the same size and had the same number of rooms, the big difference lay in the size of the garden, the length of the driveway and the provision, or not, of a garage. Those who had bought their properties were outraged to find a council estate 'for slum clearance tenants' so close to their desirable residences and insisted on the building of a wall to separate the two settlements. The result was that the council tenants had to make a long detour to reach their own homes, but despite repeated efforts to force its removal, the wall stood until 1959. A small piece remains in Wentworth Road.

This situation expressed the polarised social differences which were emerging in the inter-war years. The University, providing only term-time work, lost its monopoly of employment. The new housing was inhabited by the workforce of the car industry, construction workers and by the 2,700 employed in the civil service, a new twist to the county's tradition of service to government. The car itself, the cheapest model in 1933 priced at £122 10s., was by no means within reach of everyone, However, it was already dictating town planning requirements, deciding road widths and the provision of turning circles in new closes, and influencing the major trunk roads, some of which were turned into dual carriageways. One such section is still in use westwards out of Henley towards Bix; another, built between 1930 and 1935, is still part of the northern by-pass to the city of Oxford between Green Road roundabout and the Banbury Road. A contemporary commented on another section, from Botley to Hinksey Hill, finished in 1932, that 'it seems to serve no useful purpose'. The motor car nevertheless forced the construction of a purpose built arterial highway, the A40 between Oxford and Witney cut in 1938.

While the motor car and the provision of small scale housing was altering the appearance of both towns and villages, the grand tradition in architecture was dying. Faringdon Folly, erected in 1935, was the last in the tradition of fanciful buildings, and one large country house was not only the last in Oxfordshire but the last in England. The fourth mansion to stand at Middleton Stoney was erected in 1938 by the fashionable, if controversial, Sir Edwin Lutyens. Others were built, on a lesser scale, particularly in the southern part of the county. Amongst them is Nuffield Place at Huntercombe, built in 1914 and altered when William Morris bought it in 1933, just before his ennoblement as Lord Nuffield. It is the substantial residence of a wealthy man which preserves the fittings and furnishings of the

1930s, though the design achieved a reduction in floor space by cutting down the impressive hall found in traditional houses. It still contained reasonably sized 'public' or reception rooms, drawing room and dining room and six bedrooms. The only intimate space was a small sitting room. The plan nevertheless retained the back stairs and provision for live-in servants, though for far fewer than previously because of the increasing number of labour-saving gadgets, for kitchen work as for almost everywhere else in the house. Morris had a strong interest in all things mechanical and his purchases are on show in the butler's pantry.

Nuffield's wealth and success had come quickly; he spread it round the area, endowing fellowships in the University, a medical block for Oxford city hospitals, and finally a graduate college, the first of eight new colleges which have enlarged the University in this century. His factories benefited both town and county, for throughout the Depression of the 1930s Oxford, as so often, bucked the national trends, this time in unemployment and poverty.

The county witnessed huge changes during the war years. Amongst the preparations made in 1939-40 against German invasion was the construction on the Oxfordshire bank of the Thames of pill boxes at every possible crossing. Milestones were removed or defaced, less energetically in the Vale than in Oxfordshire. Most radical, however, was the construction of airfields. During the rearmament of the mid-1920s Abingdon airfield and a second Ordnance Depot at Bicester had been added to the four airfields of the Great War. Two training schools, Carterton and Kidlington, were built just before 1939, when an army barracks was added to Bicester, the Officers Mess now a private Nursing Home. No fewer than twenty-two airfields were built after the start of hostilities; most were used as training, back-up or repair stations. When peace came, many reverted quickly to agricultural use. Four became permanent; Abingdon, Benson with the Air Reconnaissance Unit, Brize Norton as an RAF base with the largest hangar in Europe and Upper Heyford, said to have the longest runway in Europe, until recently one of the United States Air Force's most important strategic bases. Other airfields have changed function. Kidlington is a training station and a civil airfield, Weston on the Green a commercial gliding school. At Enstone business units and a small flying club make use of the site. Barford St John, now a signal station, where some of the earliest Rolls Royce jets were tested, stands forlorn behind its barbed wire fence; Witney became the site of a small engineering firm.

The fate of others was still more radical. Two fell victim to the new industry of gravel extraction, Stanton Harcourt and Mount Farm, near

Dorchester; on its fringe was sited the new town of Berinsfield, built in the late 1950s. Far more speedily, Harwell airfield was taken over on 1 January 1946 as the headquarters of the Atomic Energy Commission. The decision to site it here was the precursor of other development in the south of the county, such as the transformation of the Culham airfield buildings into additional laboratories for nuclear research. The site is now the home of the European JET/TORUS project. The effect on the nearby towns of Abingdon and Wantage, for example, was immediate. The population increased; schools and housing had to be provided, the earliest of the successive waves of domestic building seen in the post-war county.

Much of the earliest post-war rebuild was centred on the Vale, where overspill housing from bomb-damaged London and from Reading was located. Further development followed in the 1960s. At Didcot a power station replaced the former Ordnance Depot on a site considered ideal because the railway would bring coal and Thames water would cool the six cooling towers. These were placed in two groups of three rather than as a block of six in an attempt to avoid dominating the landscape, a difficult feat since each tower is higher than the dome of St Paul's cathedral.

In the mid-sixties Dr Beeching's closure of the railway lines of rural England left Oxfordshire with only four of the nine lines built little over a century before; the London-Bristol line through the Vale, the London-Oxford-Worcester route, the London-Bicester-Banbury and Oxford-Birmingham lines. His policy left the region largely reliant on a single mode of transport, the motor vehicle, and destroyed, quite literally, the most significant advance in communications of the previous century. Although the implications were not fully appreciated at the time, the Beeching Plan meant also that there would have to be changes within every population centre, large and small alike. In Oxford a plan to cut a relief road to take traffic away from the city centre cross roads was eventually defeated, not before it had split Town and Gown, as so often in the past. A solution was found by extending the existing bypasses to form a complete circle round the city and creating partial inner ring roads, with new bridges at Marston and Donnington.

Further, and more dramatic, changes came in Oxford when the City Council bulldozed almost a quarter of the medieval city to build the Westgate Centre and its ancillary car parks. Those whose houses were destroyed were rehoused on a large estate, Blackbird Leys, five miles from the city centre. At the time this was the largest such development in the south of England, consisting of 2370 dwellings; nevertheless, it was built without schools or shops, let alone church or community centres.

Together, provision of housing and the needs of the motor vehicle are the factors which have most recently shaped Oxfordshire towns. Despite the existence of a small-scale industrial estate on the outskirts, to which Birds was attracted in 1965, Banbury, like Oxford, went in for destruction of its centre in the attempt to modernise. Its cattle market was until recently the largest in Europe, sited there because of good rail communications supplemented now by the M40, from which much has been expected. Bicester too expanded rapidly in the 1960s and 1970s, removing most of its original centre in the process. Elsewhere, industrial and housing estates notwithstanding, the small town centres have retained more of their character. None, however, is without its one-way system.

Towns and villages now share a common characteristic – infill building. In Oxford the colleges have proved particularly adept at fitting new buildings into existing space; some of the best examples are to be seen at St John's, Brasenose and University College. These contrast strongly to the controversial block development of Gloucester Green or the Seacourt Tower at Botley, both of which change the scale of urban building, another twentieth century feature. Oxford's John Radcliffe Hospital gleams white on Headington Hill, visible for miles around; the Kraft Jacobs Suchard factory at Banbury alternately steams and glitters while Wallingford's grain siloes stick out like the proverbial sore thumbs. In villages, new houses in materials brought from outside the county, make the twentieth century's contribution to the landscape clear.

Fortunately, after a short period in which decaying buildings of all types could be pulled down, preservation, not only in the form of Conservation Orders, but in the form of conversion and reuse of older buildings, is now the order of the day. Abingdon has preserved Morland's brewery and Benson an old coaching inn for use as flats, right in the centre of town; the Bliss Mill at Chipping Norton has been similarly converted. Nonconformist chapels, approximately half of which have been sold off, show a variety of ingenious reshaping into residences; even churches are following the same route. The Old Vicarage, The Old Parsonage and The Old School are increasingly common house names.

The monuments of this century make themselves obvious; War Memorials to the dead of two World Wars, electricity pylons, TV transmitters, satellite saucers. Nevertheless, many of the themes of this century repeat those of the past. Large tracts of farmland once again resemble the open fields of the middle ages, where at Great Milton, Hatford and Swalcliffe Heath the hedges of the eighteenth-century enclosers have been ripped up to allow access to large machines. Once more, new crops are being planted; maize, brilliant yellow oilseed rape, pale blue linseed and even sunflowers. The traditional groupings of farm house and buildings sometimes lie amidst huge metal barns, granaries and siloes. Some have been created for specialised agricultural enterprises; others have been converted to dwellings.

The pace of change is perhaps best expressed in the virtual disappearance of Morris's factories in Cowley, where buildings covering 344 acres (139 ha) were largely rased to the ground in 1992, only some seventy years after their construction. In the same space of time, the county has lost most of its traditional industries and its workforce is no longer largely agricultural but computer oriented. The city, its brief flirtation with heavy industry over, has returned to its traditional occupation, education, with the addition of a second university, Oxford Brookes, the development of a multitude of research centres and the establishment of innumerable language schools.

Decisions being taken now, based on the County Council's Structure Plan, will inevitably shape the way which the twenty-first century will follow. Existing urban centres may be enlarged or smaller ones revitalised and returned to some of their former importance. A new town may be created, centred on the former air base at Upper Heyford, or the clock turned back to greater rail travel. One thing is certain. The diversity of the county will not disappear.

The M40 motorway, the latest change in the county's lines of communication, has given us new perspectives on the ancient topography of the county. As the M40 emerges from the Chiltern beechwoods to slide down the Chiltern escarpment a vista from Thame to Faringdon Clumps, seen over the top of Didcot's cooling towers, spreads out. The road plunges on across Otmoor, then races uphill close to the Saxon meeting place of Bullingdon hundred before, leaving Banbury to one side, it slides out into Warwickshire. In three quarters of an hour and some forty miles, it traverses the kaleidoscope of Oxfordshire's history.

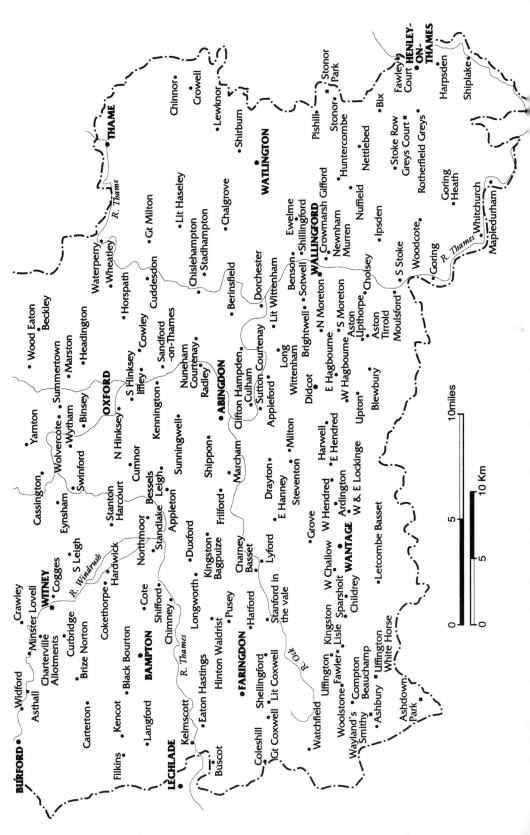

How to Get There

As a general rule Oxfordshire houses are open on one day in the week and Saturdays, Sundays and Bank Holiday Mondays from April to September. Arrangements vary and it is best to check. Most are privately owned; some are in the care of English Heritage or the National Trust. Careful planning is needed to get the most from a single week's stay. Many churches are locked; a key is usually at the vicarage.

PREHISTORY

Badbury Camp – Approx 3 m SW of Faringdon, N off B4019. Signposted circular walk. Open year round.

Blewburton fort – I m. walk E of village of Blewbury. Open all year round. No car access.

Dyke Hills Dorchester – approx ½ m. S of town beyond car park by bridge. Open year round. No cars.

Hoar Stone – ½ m S from Enstone, itself 4 m SE of Chipping Norton on A44.

Ilbury fort – ½ m S off B 4031 beyond Hempton, signposted Nether Worton. Thereafter footpath signs. Open year round. No cars.

Ridgeway – well signposted at all points where it crosses main roads, A34, B4507 or from B4000. Open year round. Walking only.

Rollright Stone, King's Men – 3 m N of Chipping Norton, W turn off A3400. None too close to villages of same name. Open year round.

Uffington White Horse – 6 m SE of Shrivenham. EH. Well signposted off B4000. Open year round. Car parking but thereafter walkers only.

Wayland's Smithy – 4 m SE of Shrivenham. EH. Signed from B4057 (small car park) or walkable from Uffington White Horse car parks. Open year round, No car access.

ROMAN

Dorchester — A slight rise in the ground along Watling Lane marks the line of the town ramparts.

North Leigh – Villa sited at East End, E of village, I m N off A4095. EH site, open year round though the building which protects the single mosaic open only one day each month April to September. Information posted at site or phone 0117-9750700.

ANGLO-SAXON

Langford church – 5 m NW of Faringdon, E off A361.

Lew Barrow – Reached by a footpath W from N end of village.

Oxford, St Michael at Northgate – Cornmarket. Seasonal opening of tower.

Wallingford, defences – Earth banks surround Kinecroft and Bullcroft, easily seen and approached from Flint House Museum. Open year round.

Waterperry church – 2 m E of Wheatley, NE off M40, signed to Garden Centre. Church within gardens.

MEDIEVAL

Broughton – 3 m SW of Banbury, W off B4035. 01295 262624.

Culham Bridge – 1 m S of Abingdon. First turn signed Culham off A415; immediately R signed footpath leads to bridge. Limited layby parking.

Deddington castle – E end of village, E off A4260. EH signposted. Open year round. Walkers only.

Deserted village sites – some of these sites require considerable imagination. Thomley (SP631090) where Thomley Hall Farm incorporates part of the earliest building; Brookend in Chastleton (SP240310); Broadstone in Enstone (SP353252); Widford, where the church is the only survival from the village; Water Eaton, NW of Oxford where the manor & chapel mark the original centre.

Ewelme – 2 m E of Benson, N off A4130. Church & Almshouses open year round, occasional Open Days at School.

Godstow nunnery – in Port Meadow; walk down the river bank from the Trout Inn, Godstow or upstream from the city. Buses to Wolvercote.

Great Coxwell Barn – 1 m SW of Faringdon, S off B4019. NT. Open year round.

Greys Court – 2 m W of Henley, between A4130 (west turn at Bix) and B481 (east turn at Bolts Green). NT. 01491 628529. Badly signposted.

Henley, School House – Access only through St Mary's Church and by appointment.

Iffley church – 2 m SE of Oxford, W turn off A4158. Summer afternoon openings, exterior any time.

Minster Lovell – 3 m W of Witney N off B4047. EH. Open year round. 01993 775315. Poor parking.

Oxford castle – in New Road. Occasional opportunities to climb the mound. Inquire at Tourist Office.

Oxford town wall – best remaining section in New College gardens. Year round access when college open.

Stanton Harcourt – 4 m SE of Witney, S of B4449. Well spaced summer openings. Inquire at Tourist Offices or direct 01865 881928.

Steventon, Priory Cottages – Corner of the Causeway and Mill Street; Steventon is 4 m S of Abingdon on B4017. The Great Hall. April-Sept Weds 2-6 by written appointment with NT tenant. Unsuitable for large groups.

Stonor Park – 4 m N of Henley, E off B480. 01491 638587.

Swalcliffe Barn – In the village 5 miles SW of Banbury on B4035. Open Sundays and BH Easter–Oct; Sats June, July, August. 01295 788278 or 259855.

Wallingford Castle – open 10-6 April-Oct.

REFORMATION TO CIVIL WAR

Abingdon Abbey – lies beyond gatehouse on E side of market place. Open year round.

Broughton – see previous section.

Chalgrove Monument – to civil war battle. NE turn, signed, off B480 10 m S of Oxford.

Chastleton House – 5 m NW of Chipping Norton, W off A44. NT. Opening date not yet known, expected soon.

Deserted villages – Eaton Hastings, NW of Faringdon, N off A417; the site lay around the church which survives; Hampton Gay, SW of Bletchingdon, off B4027. More acurately a shrunken village which lay between the cottages and the burnt out manor house.

Kelmscott – 3 m W of Faringdon W off A4095. 01367 252486.

Mapledurham – 3 m NW of Caversham, W turn off A4074 at Chazey Heath. 01734 723350.

Rycote Chapel – SE of Thame, N turn off A329. EH. Open one Sunday per month April–September. 0117 9750700.

Stonor Park – see previous section.

Wroxton Abbey – 3 m W of Banbury S of A422. Occasional garden openings providing excellent view of house. Foot access only. 01295 730551.

Carfax Conduit in Nuneham Park – this is only visible from the river.

COMMONWEALTH, RESTORATION AND COMMEMORATION

Ashdown Park – 5 m SE of Shrivenham, W off B4000, signposted. NT, timed tours only. Park open year round. 01488 72584.

Blenheim Palace – in Woodstock village 8 m NW of Oxford off A44. Buses. 01993 811235.

Buscot Parsonage – 1 m W of Buscot village beside church on A417. Can be visited by written arrangement with the NT tenant on Wednesday afternoons Easter–September. Postcode SN7 8DQ.

Coleshill – the site of the house has been laid out in flowers in the garden of The Clock House, Coleshill, 3 m SW of Faringdon on B4019. Open days or by appointment, 01793 762476.

Fawley Court, Henley – March–Oct Weds, Thurs, Sun 2-5. Museum of Polish documents in two rooms of the house. 01491 574917.

Kingston Bagpuize – 1 m S of village, 8 m W of Abingdon on A415. 01865 820259.

Kingston Lisle – 3 m W of Wantage, N off B4507. Occasional openings. 01367 820599.

Milton Manor – In Milton village 3 m S of Abingdon, S off B4016. Buses. Timed tours only. 01235 831871.

GEORGIAN AND REGENCY

Ardington House – 2 m E of Wantage, S off A417. 01235 833244.

Buscot House – 3 m NW of Faringdon on A 417. Signposted. NT. 01367 242094.

Claydon Locks – beyond village, 7 m N of Banbury E off A423.

Follies – The Eyecatcher, Rousham is actually approached by a footpath at the S end of Steeple Aston. **The Drayton Archway,** two round towers supporting a ruinated archway, was part of the landscaping at Wroxton. It lies close to a footpath S from Drayton, signed as the Banbury Circular Walk.

Rousham House – 5 m S of Deddington E off A4260. Also by rail to Lower Heyford then 1½ m walk. Occasional buses from Oxford and Banbury. Gardens open all year round. House summer only. 01869 347110.

Shotover House – gardens only. 6 m E of Oxford off A40. Buses. For dates inquire at Tourist Offices.

Wroxton – see Reformation section.

Swinford Bridge – on the B4044 between Oxford and Eynsham.

Tadpole Bridge – due S from Bampton, road signed Buckland, Pusey.

Wheatley Mill – 6 m E of Oxford on A40. Drive S through village up Ladder Hill & Windmill Lane. 3rd turning N. Open in May and one Sunday in August, otherwise by appointment; 01865 874610.

VICTORIAN AND EDWARDIAN

Banbury, the Cross – erected in 1859, the idea coming no doubt from the existence of three earlier crosses, smashed in the 17th century. Sited at crossroads A4260 & B4035.

Charney Bassett mill – in village, W turn off A338 at East Hanney. Admission of groups of at least eight by arrangement, 01235 868677.

Combe mill – N turn off A4095, or signs to Combe Halt. Open 3rd Sunday in May, August, October. 01993 891785.

Maharajah's Well – in Stoke Row village, 2 m NW off B481 at Sonning Common. Open year round.

Oxford, Martyrs' Memorial – St Giles. Erected 1841-43 to a design of George Gilbert Scott as a memorial to the leaders of the Reformation, burnt to death in 1555-56.

Venn Mill – 5 m N of Wantage on A338. Open 2nd Sunday in month April –October. 01367 718888.

Wheatley Lock-up – in village, 6 m E of Oxford, S turn off A40, by playing fields.

TWENTIETH CENTURY

Didcot Power Station – Parties by arrangement with National Power. 01235 815111.

Faringdon Folly – E side of Faringdon, steep footpath from Stanford Road. Accessible year round, occasional summer openings, no car access.

Nuffield Place – 6 m NW of Henley, NE off A4130, best found by following signs to Huntercombe Young Offenders' Camp. 01491 641224.

Tooley's Boatyard, Banbury – Open days in Feb, May, Sept, Oct; groups by appointment. 01295 261221.

MUSEUMS

A brochure listing Oxfordshire Museums and current opening times is issued annually by Thames Transit in conjunction with Oxfordshire County Council.

Oxford, Ashmolean Museum, Beaumont St. – daily (not Mons), closed Christmas, Easter, early Sept. 01865 278000.

Oxford, Museum of Oxford, Town Hall – closed Sun, Mon. 01865 815559.

Fletcher's House, Woodstock – Expected to reopen in stages from Easter 1997 after major refurbishment. 01993 811456.

Cogges Manor Farm Museum, Witney –Easter–Nov, daily. 01993 772602.

Bishop's Palace, Church Green, Witney - Sats, Suns April–Sept or by arrangement with the Cogges Museum.

Banbury Museum, The Horsefair – April–Sept Tues-Sat 01295 259855.

Wantage, Vale & Downland Museum, Church Street – Tues–Sats, Sun afternoon year round. 01235 771447.

Claydon, Museum of Bygones – Year round daily; check times, 01295 690258.

Burford, Tolsey – Easter–Nov, pm daily; May–Sept, Fri, Sat, Sun & BH 11-2. 01367 81294.

Charlbury – Easter–Oct Suns 2–4; Bank Hol Mons, 2–4. 01608 810060.

Abingdon County Hall, Market Place - Tues–Sun year round. 01235 523703.

Wallingford, Flint House – Tues–Sat March–Nov, also Suns June–Aug. 01491 835065.

Dorchester, Abbey Museum – Easter & April–Oct, weekends; May–Sept also Tues–Sat. 01865 340056.

Bloxham, Village Museum – Easter-Sept Suns and Bank Hols; Oct Sundays, Nov–Easter, 2nd Sun in month pms. 01295 720283.

Uffington, Tom Brown's School – Easter–Oct weekends, Bank Holidays 2-5 or by arrangement. 01367 820259.

Filkins, Swinford Museum – May-Sept, first Sun 2–5 or by appointment 01367 860334.

TOURIST INFORMATION OFFICES

Abingdon – 01235 522711
Banbury – 01295 259855
Burford – 01993 823558
Chipping Norton – 01608 644379
Faringdon – 01367 242191
Henley – 01491 578034
Oxford – 01865 726871
Thame – 01844 212834
Wallingford – 01491 826972
Witney – 01993 775802
Woodstock – 01993 811038

Some of the most interesting . . .

CHURCHES

Almost all Oxfordshire's churches offer some point of interest. This list identifies those most representative of one period.

North Leigh
Blewbury
Cassington
Iffley
Letcombe Bassett
Uffington
Broughton
East Hendred
Combe
Ewelme
Minster Lovell
Rycote
Sunningwell
Besselsleigh
Shrivenham
Chiselhampton
Banbury, St Mary
Oxford, SS Philip and James
    St Barnabas, Jericho
Leafield

CHAPELS

Aston Tirrold
Barford St Michael
Black Bourton
Chadlington
Charlbury
Cote by Bampton
Drayton by Abingdon
Launton
Stonesfield
Watlington

ALMSHOUSES

Abingdon
Burford
Childrey
Chipping Norton
Goring Heath
Harwell
Henley
Lyford
Spelsbury
Steeple Aston
Wantage
Witney

SCHOOLS

Ambrosden
Bampton – now the public library
Bloxham
East Hendred – private house
Henley – see How to Get There
Kingham Hill
Lewknor
Radley College
Sibford Ferris
Steeple Aston – private house
Thame – now the offices of Booker Fitch in Church Lane
Uffington – see How to get There
West Hendred – private house

Suggestions for Further Reading

Blair, W. John, *Anglo-Saxon Oxfordshire*, 1993

Bloxham, Christine, *Portrait of Oxfordshire*, 1982

Bond, James & Over, Luke, Ordnance Survey Historical Guides *Oxfordshire and Berkshire*, 1988

Cake and Cockhorse, the Journal of the Banbury History Society

Eddershaw, G D H, *The Civil War in Oxfordshire*, 1995

Emery, Frank, *The Oxfordshire Landscape*, 1974

Falkner, John Meade, *Oxfordshire*, 1899

Havinden, Mark A., *Estate Villages: a study of the Berkshire villages of Ardington and Lockinge*, 1966

Jerome, Jerome K., *Three Men in a Boat*, 1889

Jessup, Mary, *A History of Oxfordshire*, 1975

Jope, E.M. in Darby, H.C. and Campbell, E.M.J.,(eds.) *The Domesday Geography of South-East England*, 1962

Leland, John, *Itinerary*, (ed.), L. Toulmin-Smith, 1906-10

Martin,A.F. & Steel, R.W, *The Oxford Region*, 1954

McClatchey, D. *Oxfordshire Clergy*, 1777-1869, 1960

Morris Christopher, (ed.), *The Journeys of Celia Fiennes*, 1947

Oxfordshire Museum Services, Pamphlets

Oxfordshire Record Society volumes

Oxoniensia

Pevsner, Nikolaus, *The Buildings of England: Oxfordshire* 1974; Berkshire 1972

Pilling, Gordon, *Oxfordshire Houses*, 1991

Plot, Robert, *The Natural History of Oxfordshire*, 1676

Rodwell, Kirsty, (ed.), *Historic Towns of Oxfordshire*, 1975

Sherwood, Jennifer, *A Guide to the Churches of Oxfordshire*, 1989

Steane, John, *Oxfordshire*, 1996. This has a very good bibliography

Thompson, Flora, *From Lark Rise to Candleford*, 1945

Victoria County History, Oxfordshire, Berkshire

Wood-Jones, Raymond B. *Traditional Domestic Architecture in†the Banbury Region*, 1963

Young, Arthur, *A General View of the Agriculture of Oxfordshire*, 1809 and reprint 1969

Ordnance Survey Landranger maps, sheets 164, 151, 163, 165, 174, 175 cover the county.

Index